FAST FLAVOR

Great Recipes Under 35 Minutes

Cooking Arts Collection™

Cooking Club of America
12301 Whitewater Drive
Minnetonka, MN 55343
www.cookingclub.com

CONTENTS

INTRODUCTION

Let's admit it: As much as we cooks love getting creative in the kitchen, there are times when it's hard to find the time to cook something special. We're just too busy rushing to work, running dozens of errands, or chauffeuring the kids to sports, music lessons, or friends' houses. So, instead of enjoying a home-cooked meal, we settle for take-out or something out of a box or can.

It doesn't have to be that way.

With just a little bit of time and the right recipes, you can make the kinds of flavorful food that you and your family will really enjoy eating.

And where can you find these magic, time-saving recipes?

Right here in this book.

Within these pages are 75 tasty and creative dishes that are quick and easy to make. Each of the recipes featured here has been carefully developed so it can be prepared in 35 minutes or less—without compromising flavor or quality. Best of all, this book nicely blends classic comfort foods with innovative new treats, so there's sure to be meals both you and your family will like. There are hearty soups and tangy salads, quick skillet dishes, light and lively pastry and poultry, even savory side dishes and desserts to satisfy your sweet tooth.

Need more incentive to try these ideas? How about your health? All the recipes in this book have been designed to reduce fat, cholesterol, and salt. So you and your family not only get quick and flavorful meals, you get ones that are good for you as well.

Imaginative, homestyle meals that are fun to make, delicious, and healthy too. It's enough to make your mouth water just thinking about them, isn't it?

Turn the page and let your adventure begin.

PART 1
Soups & Salads

CALICO SLAW WITH POPPYSEED DRESSING

⅓ cup nonfat mayonnaise

1 tablespoon frozen orange juice concentrate

2 teaspoons fresh lemon juice

1 teaspoon poppy seeds

½ teaspoon honey

¼ teaspoon freshly ground black pepper

1½ cups finely shredded green cabbage

1½ cups finely shredded red cabbage

½ cup thinly sliced red bell peppers

½ cup stringed and julienne-cut snow peas

¼ cup coarsely grated carrot

Poppyseed dressing is usually associated with fruit salads, but this citrusy-sweet version is also tasty on a colorful toss of cabbage, peppers, snow peas and carrots. To bring out the flavor of the poppy seeds, cook them in a dry skillet over medium heat just until they smell toasty. Immediately transfer the seeds to a plate and let them cool a bit before adding them to the dressing.

1 In a salad bowl, combine the mayonnaise, orange juice concentrate, lemon juice, poppy seeds, honey and black pepper; whisk together until well blended.

2 Add the green and red cabbages, bell peppers, snow peas and carrots; toss until the vegetables are well coated with the dressing.

Preparation time 25 minutes • **Total time** 25 minutes • **Per serving** 55 calories, 0.5 g. fat (8% of calories), 0 g. saturated fat, 0 mg. cholesterol, 150 mg. sodium, 2.1 g. dietary fiber, 49 mg. calcium, 1 mg. iron, 70 mg. vitamin C, 1.6 mg. beta-carotene • **Serves 4**

❧ ❧ ❧

Cut the head of cabbage in half lengthwise, through its core.

Remove the wedge-shaped core section from each cabbage half.

Halve each half again, then lay each quarter flat on a board and shred it crosswise.

WARM CHICKEN AND ORZO SALAD

6 ounces orzo or other small pasta

1¾ cups defatted reduced-sodium chicken broth

½ cup water

12 ounces boneless, skinless chicken breasts, trimmed and cut into 1-inch chunks

4 cups broccoli florets

¼ cup packed Italian parsley sprigs

2 tablespoons extra-virgin olive oil

2 tablespoons red wine vinegar

1 tablespoon Dijon mustard

¼ teaspoon salt

½ teaspoon freshly ground black pepper

1 garlic clove, peeled

¼ cup diced, drained roasted red peppers (from a jar)

Pasta salads, often party fare, also make delightful family dinners. This one starts with the tried-and-true pairing of chicken and rice, but the "rice" is really orzo, a grain-shaped pasta. The dish tastes best when served warm, but if necessary, you can prepare it ahead of time and refrigerate it. Just be sure to take the salad out of the refrigerator a little while before serving time so that it can return to room temperature.

1 Bring a covered medium saucepan of water to a boil over high heat. Add the pasta to the boiling water, return to a boil and cook for 8 to 10 minutes or according to package directions until al dente. Drain in a colander, rinse briefly under cold running water and drain again. Transfer the pasta to a large salad bowl.

2 While the pasta is cooking, bring 1½ cups of the broth and the water to a boil in a medium skillet. Add the chicken and return to a boil. Reduce the heat to medium-low, cover and simmer, stirring occasionally, for 6 to 8 minutes, or until the chicken is cooked through. Using a slotted spoon, transfer the chicken to the bowl of orzo; reserve the broth in the skillet.

3 Return the broth to a boil over high heat. Add the broccoli and return to a boil. Cook for 3 to 5 minutes, or until the broccoli is crisp-tender. Drain the broccoli in a colander, cool briefly under cold running water and drain again. Add the broccoli to the bowl of orzo.

4 Combine the parsley, oil, vinegar, mustard, salt, black pepper and the remaining ¼ cup broth in a food processor. With the processor running, drop the garlic clove through the feed tube; process the mixture until puréed.

5 Pour the dressing over the pasta mixture. Add the roasted peppers and toss the salad to mix well. Serve warm.

Preparation time 10 minutes • **Total time** 20 minutes • **Per serving** 365 calories, 9.4 g. fat (23% of calories), 1.4 g. saturated fat, 49 mg. cholesterol, 400 mg. sodium, 5.8 g. dietary fiber, 83 mg. calcium, 4 mg. iron, 109 mg. vitamin C, 2 mg. beta-carotene • **Serves 4**

❧ ❧ ❧

BLACK BEAN SOUP

2 cans (19 ounces each) black beans, rinsed and drained

1¾ cups defatted low-sodium chicken broth

1 cup water

1 teaspoon ground cumin

¼ teaspoon dried oregano

¼ teaspoon freshly ground black pepper

Large pinch of ground red pepper

1 teaspoon olive oil

½ large red bell pepper, slivered

½ large green bell pepper, slivered

½ teaspoon grated lemon zest

Bean soups, from sustaining Yankee bean to savory Italian mine-strone, find favor all over the world. If you'd like to make this soup with dried black beans, place 1 pound of beans in a large pot with cold water to cover; refrigerate overnight. Drain the beans, cover with fresh water, and simmer for 1¼ hours, or until tender. You'll have enough for this recipe, plus leftovers for other dishes.

1 In a large, heavy saucepan, combine the beans, broth, water, cumin, oregano, black pepper and ground red pepper. Cover and bring to a boil over high heat. Reduce the heat to low and simmer, stirring once or twice, for 15 minutes, or until the flavors are blended.

2 Meanwhile, in a small no-stick skillet, warm the oil over medium-high heat. Add the bell peppers, reduce the heat to medium and sauté for 4 to 6 minutes, or until tender.

3 Ladle half of the soup into a food processor or blender and process until puréed (work in batches if necessary). Return the purée to the pan; add the lemon zest.

4 Ladle the soup into bowls and top each serving with some of the sautéed bell peppers.

Preparation time 15 minutes • **Total time** 35 minutes • **Per serving** 182 calories, 3.1 g. fat (15% of calories), 0.4 g. saturated fat, 0 mg. cholesterol, 460 mg. sodium, 7.8 g. dietary fiber, 62 mg. calcium, 4 mg. iron, 38 mg. vitamin C, 0.3 mg. beta-carotene • **Serves 4**

To soak dried beans, place them in a pot or bowl and add cold water to cover.

After soaking, simmer the beans in fresh water, skimming the foam as they cook.

MEXICAN TACO SALAD

4 corn tortillas

8 ounces lean, trimmed beef top round

1 tablespoon chili powder

½ teaspoon olive oil

2 tablespoons defatted beef broth

1 large tomato, diced

1 can (10½ ounces) pinto beans or red kidney beans, rinsed and drained

1 tablespoon chopped, seeded canned jalapeño chilies (optional)

2 cups shredded iceberg lettuce

1 small red onion, sliced

1 tablespoon fresh lime juice

1½ ounces Cheddar cheese, shredded

¼ cup chopped fresh cilantro

You're far better off making a taco salad at home than ordering one at a fast-food restaurant. Served with a deep-fried flour tortilla, cheese, sour cream and dressing, one popular fast-food taco salad packs about 900 calories and 60 grams of fat—a terrific incentive to shop for some lean, flavorful ingredients and assemble this beefy salad in your own kitchen.

1 Preheat the oven to 400°.

2 Stack the tortillas and cut them into 8 wedges each. Arrange the tortilla wedges in a single layer on a baking sheet and bake for 8 to 10 minutes, or until crisp and lightly browned. Remove the baking sheet from the oven and let the tortilla chips cool on the baking sheet.

3 While the tortilla chips are baking, cut the beef into cubes and process in a food processor until finely ground. Add the chili powder and pulse just until mixed.

4 In a medium no-stick skillet, warm the oil over high heat until hot but not smoking. Crumble in the beef, add the broth and sauté for 2 to 3 minutes, or until the meat is no longer pink. Add the tomatoes, beans and jalapeños, if using, and sauté for 3 to 4 minutes, or until the tomatoes are softened and the mixture is just heated through.

5 Arrange the shredded lettuce and onions in a shallow serving bowl; drizzle with the lime juice. Spoon the beef mixture on top and sprinkle the Cheddar over it. Scatter the tortilla chips around the beef and sprinkle with the cilantro.

Preparation time 15 minutes • **Total time** 35 minutes • **Per serving** 249 calories, 7.5 g. fat (27% of calories), 3.1 g. saturated fat, 44 mg. cholesterol, 310 mg. sodium, 5.2 g. dietary fiber, 172 mg. calcium, 3 mg. iron, 18 mg. vitamin C, 1 mg. beta-carotene • **Serves 4**

Stack the tortillas and cut them in half, then stack the two halves and cut them into wedges.

ON THE MENU
Accompany the taco salad with your favorite bottled salsa. Offer a refreshing pitcher of pink lemonade, made by mixing a small amount of cranberry juice into fresh lemonade. For a dessert with Mexican flair, dust scoops of chocolate frozen yogurt with ground cinnamon.

LEMON-DILL SHRIMP CAESAR

12 slices (3½ ounces) Italian or
   French bread, cut ½-inch thick

3 garlic cloves (1 halved and
   2 minced)

¼ cup buttermilk

3 tablespoons chopped fresh dill

1 ounce Romano cheese, coarsely
   grated

½ teaspoon anchovy paste

¼ teaspoon freshly ground black
   pepper

1 pound medium shrimp, peeled
   and deveined, with tails attached

2 teaspoons extra-virgin olive oil

½ teaspoon grated lemon zest

6 cups Romaine lettuce, torn into
   bite-size pieces

2 cups stemmed and halved
   cherry tomatoes

1 bunch watercress or arugula,
   tough stems removed

8 ounces small fresh mushrooms,
   sliced

Lemon slices, for garnish
(optional)

Caesar salad has made a major comeback in the past few years after having been out of fashion for a decade or two: This classic salad is now turning up on restaurant menus nationwide. For an update, still-warm broiled shrimp, savory with a garlic-lemon marinade, are tossed with Romaine, watercress, cherry tomatoes and mushrooms. The dressing is a creamy dilled Caesar, minus the egg.

1 Preheat the broiler. Rub the bread slices with the halved garlic. Place the bread in a jelly-roll pan and broil 4 to 5 inches from the heat for 2 minutes per side, or until toasted. Transfer the bread from the pan to a plate, leaving the broiler on.

2 To make the dressing, in a large bowl, whisk together the buttermilk, dill, Romano, anchovy paste and black pepper; set aside.

3 Place the shrimp in the jelly-roll pan and sprinkle with the olive oil, minced garlic and lemon zest. Toss the shrimp to coat evenly and arrange in a single layer in the pan. Broil the shrimp 4 to 5 inches from the heat, turning once, for 3 to 4 minutes, or until opaque.

4 Meanwhile, add the Romaine, tomatoes, watercress or arugula and mushrooms to the bowl with the dressing and toss to mix. Add the broiled shrimp and toss gently. Divide the salad among 4 plates and serve with 3 bread slices each. Garnish with lemon slices, if desired.

Preparation time 25 minutes • **Total time** 35 minutes • **Per serving** 267 calories, 7.5 g. fat (25% of calories), 1 g. saturated fat, 148 mg. cholesterol, 441 mg. sodium, 4.6 g. dietary fiber, 257 mg. calcium, 5 mg. iron, 51 mg. vitamin C, 2.7 mg. beta-carotene • **Serves 4**

FOR A CHANGE
Romaine is the usual lettuce for Cobb salad, but you could use Bibb, Boston or mesclun (a mix of colorful baby lettuce leaves) instead of the watercress or arugula called for here.

HEAD START
You can wash and dry the greens ahead of time; refrigerate them in loosely closed plastic bags. Make the dressing in advance, too, and refrigerate it in a tightly closed jar.

HEARTY CHICKEN AND GREENS SOUP

1 medium leek

2 cups water

1¾ cups defatted reduced-sodium chicken broth

8 ounces boneless, skinless chicken breasts, cut crosswise into ½-inch-thick strips

1 cup frozen chopped leaf spinach

2 large carrots, sliced

2 garlic cloves, minced

½ teaspoon dried thyme, crumbled

¼ teaspoon salt

¼ teaspoon freshly ground black pepper

3 ounces thin egg noodles

2 tablespoons chopped fresh Italian parsley

Chicken soup may really be good for a cold (scientific research has shown that its steamy heat does help clear your head). Medicinal properties aside, however, a bowl of this home-made soup, brimming with chunks of chicken, vegetables and egg noodles, seems to make everyone feel better, especially on a chilly autumn or winter evening.

1 Halve the leek lengthwise and rinse each half well under cold running water. Cut the leek halves crosswise into ½-inch pieces.

2 In a large, heavy saucepan, combine the leeks, water, broth, chicken strips, spinach, carrots, garlic, thyme, salt and black pepper. Cover and bring to a boil over high heat. Reduce the heat to low and simmer for 8 minutes.

3 Stir in the noodles, increase the heat to medium-high and return to a boil. Reduce the heat to medium-low, cover and simmer, stirring occasionally, for 4 to 6 minutes, or until the noodles, vegetables and chicken are tender.

4 Remove the pan from the heat and stir in the parsley.

Preparation time 10 minutes • **Total time** 35 minutes • **Per serving** 217 calories, 2.5 g. fat (10% of calories), 0.4 g. saturated fat, 53 mg. cholesterol, 523 mg. sodium, 3.9 g. dietary fiber, 121 mg. calcium, 4 mg. iron, 26 mg. vitamin C, 11 mg. beta-carotene • **Serves 4**

To clean leeks, first cut off the coarse parts of the green tops (leave on the tender green parts for this recipe).

Sand can get caught between the layers of the leek; splitting the leek lengthwise makes it easier to wash the sand away.

Hold the split leeks under cold running water, fanning the layers to release any dirt. Wash the leaves separately.

THAI BEEF SALAD

- 12 ounces lean, trimmed boneless beef sirloin or top round steak
- 2 garlic cloves (1 halved and 1 minced)
- ¼ teaspoon freshly ground black pepper
- ¼ cup rice wine vinegar
- 2 teaspoons vegetable oil
- 1 teaspoon dark sesame oil
- 1 teaspoon sugar
- ½ teaspoon grated fresh ginger
- ¼ teaspoon salt
- ¼ teaspoon crushed red pepper flakes
- 2 scallions, thinly sliced
- 12 cups green-leaf lettuce, torn into bite-size pieces
- 1 cup thinly sliced kirby or English cucumbers
- 1 cup loosely packed fresh cilantro leaves, chopped
- 1 cup loosely packed fresh mint leaves, chopped
- 1 small ripe mango or papaya, peeled and diced
- 1 cup bean sprouts
- 2 medium carrots, cut into julienne strips
- 1 tablespoon chopped unsalted dry-roasted peanuts
- Lime wedges, for garnish (optional)

There is a category of delicious Thai salads called, appropriately enough, *yum:* These salads consist of greens topped with meat or poultry, fish or shellfish. *Yum gong,* for instance, comes with curry-flavored shrimp, while *yum pla muok* is made with spiced squid and pickled garlic. This dish is based on *yum nuer,* a salad topped with slices of spicy grilled beef. A sprinkling of fresh herbs is characteristic of *yums;* here, fresh cilantro and mint are added to the dressing instead.

1 Preheat the broiler. Spray the broiler-pan rack with no-stick spray.

2 Rub the steak on both sides with the halved garlic clove, then sprinkle with the black pepper. Place the steak on the prepared broiler-pan rack and broil 4 to 6 inches from the heat, turning once, for 5 minutes per side, or until medium rare. Transfer the steak to a plate and let stand for 5 minutes.

3 Meanwhile, make the dressing. In a large bowl, whisk together the vinegar, vegetable oil, sesame oil, sugar, ginger, salt, red pepper flakes and minced garlic.

4 Transfer the steak to a cutting board and pour any juices remaining on the steak plate into a medium bowl. Add 1 tablespoon of the dressing and the scallions to the juices, and stir to combine.

5 Carve the steak into ¼-inch-thick slices. Add the steak to the bowl with the scallions and toss to coat.

6 Add the lettuce, cucumbers, cilantro and mint to the dressing in the large bowl and toss to coat. Arrange the lettuce mixture on 4 plates. Mound the steak mixture on top, then top with the mangoes or papayas, bean sprouts and carrots. Sprinkle the salads with the chopped peanuts. Garnish with lime wedges, if desired.

Preparation time 25 minutes • **Total time** 30 minutes • **Per serving** 266 calories, 10 g. fat (34% of calories), 2.5 g. saturated fat, 57 mg. cholesterol, 211 mg. sodium, 4.2 g. dietary fiber, 166 mg. calcium, 6 mg. iron, 56 mg. vitamin C, 9.4 mg. beta-carotene • **Serves 4**

❧ ❧ ❧

SCALLOP AND ORANGE TOSS

3 medium navel oranges

1 tablespoon plus 1 teaspoon extra-virgin olive oil

1 tablespoon plus 1 teaspoon red wine vinegar

½ teaspoon grated lemon zest

¼ teaspoon freshly ground black pepper

⅛ teaspoon salt

12 cups fresh spinach leaves, tough stems removed

4 ounces radicchio, thinly sliced

1 medium red bell pepper, diced

2 ounces trimmed Canadian bacon, finely diced

⅓ cup thinly sliced shallots

1 pound sea scallops, tough muscle removed

Eye-catching radicchio is expensive, but the firm leaves of each small head are tightly packed, so there's little waste.

Because the ingredients for this salad are few and their preparation simple, it's important that everything be of the very best quality. Take an extra moment at the market to select the plumpest scallops, the heaviest, juiciest oranges and the freshest, crispest spinach; splurge a bit on the radicchio and extra-virgin olive oil. Buy some pretty dinner rolls, too, and heat them while you make the salad. When you sit down to the meal, you'll agree it was worth every minute and the few extra pennies.

1 Using a serrated knife, pare the peel and white pith from the oranges. Working over a medium bowl, cut out the sections from between the membranes and set the sections aside. Squeeze 3 tablespoons of orange juice from the membranes into the bowl.

2 To the orange juice, add 3 teaspoons of the oil, the vinegar, lemon zest, ⅛ teaspoon of the black pepper and the salt; whisk to combine.

3 In a large bowl, combine the reserved orange sections, spinach, radicchio and bell peppers.

4 In a medium no-stick skillet, warm the remaining 1 teaspoon oil over medium-high heat. Stir in the bacon and shallots, and cook for 2 minutes, or until golden. Stir in the scallops and the remaining ⅛ teaspoon black pepper, and sauté for 2 minutes, or until the scallops are opaque. With a slotted spoon, transfer the scallop mixture to a plate.

5 Add the orange dressing to the skillet and cook, stirring, for 30 seconds to warm.

6 Add the warm dressing to the bowl with the orange sections and spinach mixture, and toss to mix. Divide the spinach mixture among 4 plates and top with the scallop mixture.

Preparation time 30 minutes • **Total time** 35 minutes • **Per serving** 268 calories, 7.3 g. fat (23% of calories), 1.2 g. saturated fat, 45 mg. cholesterol, 590 mg. sodium, 7.6 g. dietary fiber, 264 mg. calcium, 6 mg. iron, 152 mg. vitamin C, 7.8 mg. beta-carotene • **Serves 4**

ASIAN CHICKEN NOODLE SOUP

- 1 **tablespoon plus 1 teaspoon vegetable oil**

- 12 **ounces skinless, boneless chicken breast halves, thinly sliced**

- 4 **scallions, thinly sliced on the diagonal**

- 2 **garlic cloves, minced**

- 1 **teaspoon grated fresh ginger**

- 2 **cups thinly sliced small white mushrooms**

- 3 **cups defatted reduced-sodium chicken broth**

- 2½ **cups water**

- ½ **cup canned sliced bamboo shoots, rinsed and drained**

- ¼ **teaspoon crushed red pepper flakes**

- 4 **ounces fresh cappellini pasta**

- 4 **cups packed fresh spinach leaves, coarsely chopped**

- 1 **tablespoon balsamic vinegar**

- 2 **tablespoons reduced-sodium soy sauce**

- 2 **large egg whites, lightly beaten**

- ½ **teaspoon dark sesame oil**

- 1 **medium carrot, shredded**

- ¼ **cup chopped fresh cilantro**

This bountiful soup is made with cappellini (angel-hair pasta) instead of Asian noodles. If you can get Chinese or Japanese noodles (shown below), try them in this soup; cook the noodles according to the package directions.

1 In a large saucepan, warm the vegetable oil over medium-high heat until very hot but not smoking. Add the chicken and stir-fry for 2 minutes, or until opaque. Add the scallions, garlic and ginger, and stir-fry for 30 seconds, or until fragrant. Add the mushrooms and stir-fry for 1 minute, or until tender.

2 Add the broth, water, bamboo shoots and red pepper flakes, and bring to a boil over high heat. Stir in the pasta and spinach, and cook for 1 minute, or until the pasta is tender and the spinach is just wilted. Reduce the heat to medium and stir in the vinegar and soy sauce. Stir in the beaten egg whites and simmer, stirring, for 1 minute. Stir in the sesame oil.

3 Ladle the soup into 4 bowls and top with the carrots and cilantro.

Preparation time 20 minutes • **Total time** 35 minutes • **Per serving** 293 calories, 7.3 g. fat (23% of calories), 1.1 g. saturated fat, 70 mg. cholesterol, 952 mg. sodium, 4.2 g. dietary fiber, 122 mg. calcium, 5 mg. iron, 31 mg. vitamin C, 6.5 mg. beta-carotene • **Serves 4**

Japanese dried noodles: *tomoshiraga somen* (fine wheat noodles), *soba* (buckwheat noodles) and *udon* (wheat noodles).

Two types of quick-cooking Chinese dried egg noodles, or *dan mian*. Those on the right are made with wheat flour.

TROPICAL CHICKEN SALAD

2 tablespoons sliced natural
    almonds

2 teaspoons ground cumin

1 cup defatted chicken broth

12 ounces skinless, boneless
    chicken breast halves, cut into
    1-inch chunks

1 tablespoon cornstarch dissolved
    in 1 tablespoon cold water

¼ cup apricot nectar

1 tablespoon fresh lime juice

1 tablespoon honey

¼ teaspoon freshly ground
    black pepper

⅛ teaspoon crushed red pepper
    flakes

2 tablespoons chopped fresh
    cilantro

2 cups fresh pineapple chunks
    (or juice-packed canned
    pineapple, drained)

    Half of a ripe papaya, peeled,
    seeded and cut into chunks
    (1 cup)

1 ripe mango, peeled and cut into
    chunks (1 cup)

4 cups (1 large bunch) watercress
    or spinach, washed and trimmed

Pineapples, with their natural "armor," have been shipped to this country since the eighteenth century, but thinner-skinned mangoes and papayas are not such good travelers. Fortunately, they're now grown in Hawaii, Florida and California, and are available in most supermarkets. When ripe, mangoes and papayas will yield to gentle pressure; if necessary, ripen them in paper bags for a few days.

1 In a heavy, medium no-stick skillet, toast the almonds over medium-high heat, tossing frequently, for about 4 minutes, or until lightly browned. Tip the almonds onto a plate to stop the cooking.

2 Add the cumin to the skillet and cook over medium heat, stirring frequently, for about 4 minutes, or until the cumin is toasted and fragrant. Immediately transfer half of the cumin to a salad bowl; pour the broth into the skillet and bring to a boil over high heat.

3 Add the chicken to the skillet and reduce the heat to medium; cover and cook, stirring frequently, for 3 to 4 minutes, or until the chicken is cooked through. With a slotted spoon, transfer the chicken to a plate; cover it with wax paper to keep it moist.

4 Increase the heat to high and bring the cooking liquid to a boil. Boil for about 3 minutes, or until the liquid is reduced to about ¼ cup. Stir in the cornstarch mixture and return to a boil, whisking constantly (the mixture will be extremely thick). Remove from the heat.

5 Scrape the thickened liquid into the salad bowl and whisk in the apricot nectar, lime juice, honey, black pepper and red pepper; continue whisking until smooth. Stir in the cilantro.

6 Add to the bowl the chicken and any juices that have collected on the plate, the pineapple, papaya and mango, and toss gently to mix.

7 Spread the watercress or spinach on a large platter. Top with the chicken salad and sprinkle with the toasted almonds.

Preparation time 25 minutes • **Total time** 35 minutes • **Per serving** 238 calories, 3.7 g. fat (14% of calories), 0.5 g. saturated fat, 49 mg. cholesterol, 322 mg. sodium, 2.7 g. dietary fiber, 90 mg. calcium, 2 mg. iron, 71 mg. vitamin C, 3 mg. beta-carotene
Serves 4

❧ ❧ ❧

COBB SALAD WITH PARMESAN DRESSING

½ cup low-fat buttermilk

3 tablespoons grated Parmesan cheese

2 tablespoons light sour cream

1 tablespoon distilled white vinegar

¾ teaspoon coarsely cracked black pepper

⅛ teaspoon salt

3 cups loosely packed torn red-leaf lettuce

1 medium head Boston lettuce, torn into bite-size pieces (about 3 cups)

1 can (16 ounces) chick-peas, rinsed and drained

4 ounces julienne-cut skinless roast turkey breast

Whites of 4 hard-cooked eggs, coarsely chopped

Half of a ripe medium avocado, cut into chunks

1½ cups halved cherry tomatoes

½ cup thinly sliced radishes

A California classic, the Cobb salad was a signature dish of the Brown Derby restaurant in Hollywood. It's a sort of salad-bar-in-a-dish, with finely chopped greens, herbs, chicken, eggs, bacon, tomatoes and blue cheese arrayed in broad bands in a big bowl. The salad is first displayed in all its multicolored glory, then tossed with a vinaigrette. Here, the components are cut into more substantial pieces and arranged on a platter; toss the salad gently before serving, or simply pour on the dressing and pass the platter around.

1 To make the dressing, in a small bowl, whisk together the buttermilk, Parmesan, sour cream, vinegar, pepper and salt.

2 Spread the red-leaf and Boston lettuces in a large, shallow bowl or on a platter. Arrange the chick-peas, turkey, egg whites, avocados, cherry tomatoes and radishes in even bands over the lettuce.

3 Drizzle the dressing over the salad, toss if desired and serve.

Preparation time 30 minutes • **Total time** 30 minutes • **Per serving** 243 calories, 8.7 g. fat (32% of calories), 2.2 g. saturated fat, 30 mg. cholesterol, 384 mg. sodium, 5.3 g. dietary fiber, 188 mg. calcium, 4 mg. iron, 30 mg. vitamin C, 1 mg. beta-carotene • **Serves 4**

Halve the avocado, then tap the blade of a heavy knife against the pit; use the knife like a screwdriver to twist out the pit.

Grasp the skin at the blossom end and pull. The skin should come off smoothly, leaving the flesh unmarked.

FRUITED CHICKEN AND COUSCOUS SALAD

½ **cup defatted chicken broth**

⅔ **cup water**

¾ **cup instant couscous**

¼ **cup slivered dried apricots**

2 **tablespoons golden raisins**

2 **medium navel oranges**

2 **tablespoons fresh lemon juice**

2 **tablespoons chopped red onion**

1 **tablespoon extra-virgin olive oil**

1 **tablespoon honey**

½ **teaspoon freshly ground black pepper**

¼ **teaspoon salt**

⅛ **teaspoon ground red pepper**

12 **ounces skinless, boneless chicken breast halves, cut crosswise into ½-inch-wide strips**

½ **teaspoon ground coriander**

1 **large red bell pepper, cut into thin strips**

½ **cup thinly sliced fennel or celery**

4 **cups colorful mixed greens, torn into bite-size pieces**

Couscous is a granular pasta made from semolina flour and water. Delicately flavored, it readily absorbs savory or sweet sauces, gravies and dressings. In Morocco, couscous is steamed slowly over a pot of spicy stew, but the instant couscous you'll find in your supermarket just needs to steep briefly in boiling liquid.

1 In a medium saucepan, bring the broth and water to a boil over high heat. Stir in the couscous, apricots and raisins, and remove the pan from the heat. Cover and let stand for 5 minutes, or until the couscous has absorbed the liquid. Spread the couscous in a shallow baking dish and place in the freezer for 10 minutes to chill.

2 Preheat the broiler. Spray a jelly-roll pan with no-stick spray.

3 Using a serrated knife, pare the peel and pith from the oranges. Working over a medium bowl, cut out the sections from between the membranes; set the sections aside. Squeeze the juice from the membranes into a large bowl: You should have about 3 tablespoons of juice.

4 To the orange juice, add 1 tablespoon of the lemon juice, the red onions, oil, honey, ¼ teaspoon of the black pepper, ⅛ teaspoon of the salt and half of the ground red pepper.

5 Place the chicken strips in the prepared pan and sprinkle with the coriander, the remaining 1 tablespoon lemon juice, remaining ¼ teaspoon black pepper, remaining ⅛ teaspoon salt and remaining ground red pepper. Toss the chicken to season evenly.

6 Broil the chicken 4 to 5 inches from the heat, turning the pieces several times, for 4 to 6 minutes, or until cooked through.

7 Add the chilled couscous, the chicken, bell peppers and fennel or celery to the dressing, and toss to mix. Add the orange sections and toss gently. Spread the greens on a platter and mound the couscous mixture in the center.

Preparation time 20 minutes • **Total time** 30 minutes • **Per serving** 363 calories, 5.5 g. fat (14% of calories), 0.3 g. saturated fat, 49 mg. cholesterol, 339 mg. sodium, 4 g. dietary fiber, 95 mg. calcium, 3 mg. iron, 106 mg. vitamin C, 2 mg. beta-carotene
Serves 4

❧ ❧ ❧

PART 2
Skillet Meals &
Stir-Fries

DOUBLE ORANGE BEEF WITH VEGETABLES

2¼ cups plus ⅓ cup water

2 cups quick-cooking brown rice

⅓ cup fresh orange juice

2 tablespoons orange marmalade

2 tablespoons reduced-sodium soy sauce

1½ teaspoons cornstarch

¼ teaspoon crushed red pepper flakes

12 ounces lean, trimmed boneless beef sirloin or top round steak, thinly sliced

½ pound fresh asparagus spears, trimmed and diagonally sliced into 1-inch pieces

2 medium carrots, thinly sliced on the diagonal

2 teaspoons vegetable oil

1 medium red bell pepper, cut into thin strips

4 ounces shiitake or white mushrooms, sliced

3 large scallions, thinly sliced on the diagonal

2 garlic cloves, minced

½ teaspoon grated fresh ginger

Rice turns this stir-fry into a well-rounded meal, and quick-cooking brown rice, used here, is a great time-saver. Alternatively, you could cook regular brown rice the night before you plan to serve this dish, then reheat it while you stir-fry the vegetables and beef. Add a little water or broth to the rice before reheating in a covered pot over gentle heat.

1 In a medium saucepan, bring 2¼ cups of the water to a boil over high heat. Stir in the rice and reduce the heat to medium-low; cover and simmer for 10 minutes, or until the rice is tender and the liquid is absorbed. Remove the pan from the heat and set aside.

2 While the rice is cooking, in a medium bowl, combine the orange juice, marmalade, soy sauce, cornstarch and red pepper flakes, stirring until smooth. Stir in the beef and let stand while you prepare the vegetables.

3 In a large no-stick skillet, bring the remaining ⅓ cup of water to a boil over medium-high heat. Add the asparagus and carrots, cover and cook for 3 minutes, or until the vegetables are just tender. Drain the vegetables in a colander and transfer to a medium bowl. Wipe the skillet dry.

4 In the dry skillet, warm 1 teaspoon of the oil over medium-high heat. Add the bell peppers and mushrooms, and stir-fry for 2 minutes, or until the vegetables are tender. Add the scallions, garlic and ginger, and stir-fry for 30 seconds, or until fragrant. Transfer to the bowl with the other vegetables.

5 Add the remaining 1 teaspoon oil to the skillet. Add the beef and the marinade, and stir-fry for 3 to 4 minutes, or until the beef is cooked through. Add the vegetables and stir-fry for 1 minute, or until the vegetables are heated through. Fluff the rice with a fork and serve with the beef and vegetables.

Preparation time 25 minutes • **Total time** 35 minutes • **Per serving** 399 calories, 8.4 g. fat (18% of calories), 1.7 g. saturated fat, 52 mg. cholesterol, 395 mg. sodium, 4.8 g. dietary fiber, 51 mg. calcium, 4 mg. iron, 70 mg. vitamin C, 7.1 mg. beta-carotene • **Serves 4**

MEDITERRANEAN-STYLE TUNA AND PASTA

1 **pint (8 ounces) cherry tomatoes, stemmed and halved**

2 **tablespoons rinsed and drained capers**

2 **tablespoons chopped fresh dill**

2 **garlic cloves, minced**

2 **teaspoons grated lemon zest**

2 **teaspoons olive oil**

½ **teaspoon salt**

½ **teaspoon freshly ground black pepper**

8 **ounces penne pasta**

1½ **pounds spinach, trimmed and chopped**

8 **ounces tuna steak, cut into 1-inch cubes**

2 **ounces feta cheese, crumbled**

The tiny, tight buds of "nonpareil" capers (on the left) are considered superior to the larger capers on the right. Nonpareils are slightly more expensive.

This meal is almost like a salad in a skillet—light and fresh and full of vegetables. In fact, you needn't rush to the table with the dish, as it would be delicious served warm, in the manner of many stylish dinner salads. The fresh tuna, tomatoes, herbs, garlic, olive oil and capers reflect its Mediterranean roots.

1 Bring a large covered pot of water to a boil over high heat.

2 In a large bowl, combine the cherry tomatoes, capers, dill, garlic, lemon zest, olive oil and ¼ teaspoon each of the salt and black pepper.

3 Add the penne to the boiling water, return to a boil and cook for 8 to 10 minutes, or according to package directions until al dente. During the last 1 minute of cooking, add the spinach. Drain the pasta and spinach together in a colander.

4 Add the pasta and spinach to the tomato mixture, and toss gently to combine.

5 Spray a large no-stick skillet with no-stick spray. Add the tuna and cook over medium-high heat for 3 to 5 minutes, or just until browned. Add the remaining ¼ teaspoon each salt and black pepper, and toss with the tuna.

6 Add the pasta and spinach mixture to the tuna in the skillet, then stir in the feta cheese; toss well. Cook for 1 minute to heat through.

Preparation time 15 minutes • **Total time** 30 minutes • **Per serving** 395 calories, 9.8 g. fat (22% of calories), 3.3 g. saturated fat, 34 mg. cholesterol, 671 mg. sodium, 5.4 g. dietary fiber, 218 mg. calcium, 7 mg. iron, 47 mg. vitamin C, 5.9 mg. beta-carotene • **Serves 4**

FOR A CHANGE
Scallops are a delicious variation on this recipe. Use 8 ounces of sea scallops; halve any that are very large. Sauté the scallops for 4 to 5 minutes, or until opaque. You can vary the seasonings, too: Fresh dill is wonderful with fish and shellfish, but you could try other fresh herbs, such as tarragon or oregano, when available.

ON THE MENU
Serve lime sorbet with fresh or frozen raspberries for a pretty, refreshing finale.

SHRIMP WITH LEMON AND ALMONDS

¼ cup fresh lemon juice

2 tablespoons rice wine vinegar

1 tablespoon plus 1 teaspoon sugar

1 teaspoon grated lemon zest

⅛ teaspoon crushed red pepper flakes

1 tablespoon plus 1 teaspoon reduced-sodium soy sauce

1 tablespoon dry sherry

2 teaspoons cornstarch

12 ounces medium shrimp, peeled and deveined, with tails attached

¼ cup blanched slivered almonds

1 tablespoon plus 1 teaspoon vegetable oil

8 ounces sugar snap peas or snow peas, trimmed

1 medium red bell pepper, diced

1 medium yellow bell pepper, diced

1 small onion, diced

2 garlic cloves, minced

2 tablespoons water

½ cup sliced water chestnuts

2 tablespoons chopped Italian parsley

6 ounces fresh cappellini pasta

Here's an eclectic meal worthy of today's hot young chefs—who often label such dishes "fusion cuisine." While many of the ingredients (soy sauce, rice wine vinegar and water chestnuts) and techniques ("velvet-coating" the shrimp with a cornstarch mixture and stir-frying) are Asian, the stir-fried shrimp and vegetables are served over cappellini pasta in classic Italian style.

1 Bring a large covered pot of water to a boil over high heat. Meanwhile, in a small bowl, whisk together the lemon juice, vinegar, sugar, lemon zest and red pepper flakes until blended; set aside.

2 In a medium bowl, whisk together the soy sauce, sherry and cornstarch until smooth. Add the shrimp and toss to coat. Refrigerate for 15 minutes.

3 Meanwhile, in a large skillet over medium-high heat, toast the almonds, tossing frequently, for 2 to 3 minutes, or until golden. Transfer to a small bowl.

4 In the large skillet, warm 2 teaspoons of the oil over medium-high heat until very hot but not smoking. Add the peas, peppers, onions and garlic, and stir-fry for 1 minute. Add the water, cover and cook for 2 minutes, or until the vegetables are just tender. Transfer to a plate.

5 In the large skillet, warm the remaining 2 teaspoons oil over medium-high heat. Add the shrimp and the marinade, and stir-fry for 5 to 6 minutes, or just until the shrimp turn pink and opaque. Stir in the lemon-juice mixture, reduce the heat to medium and simmer for 1 minute. Stir in the vegetables, water chestnuts and parsley. Sprinkle with the toasted almonds and remove the pan from the heat.

6 Add the cappellini to the boiling water; return to a boil and cook for 30 to 45 seconds, or until the pasta is al dente. Drain in a colander. Divide the pasta among 4 plates and top with the shrimp mixture.

Preparation time 25 minutes • **Total time** 30 minutes • **Per serving** 391 calories, 11.3 g. fat (26% of calories), 1.4 g. saturated fat, 136 mg. cholesterol, 378 mg. sodium, 4.3 g. dietary fiber, 121 mg. calcium, 4 mg. iron, 68 mg. vitamin C, 0.8 mg. beta-carotene • **Serves 4**

HOISIN PORK AND VEGETABLES

2 tablespoons hoisin sauce

2 tablespoons dry sherry

2 tablespoons reduced-sodium soy sauce

1 tablespoon honey

1½ teaspoons cornstarch

½ teaspoon dark sesame oil

¼ teaspoon crushed red pepper flakes

8 ounces lean, boneless pork loin, cut into ¼-inch-wide strips

8 ounces whole-wheat spaghettini

⅔ cup water

6 cups broccoli florets or 8 cups trimmed, cut-up broccoli rabe (2-inch lengths)

2 medium carrots, sliced

3 teaspoons vegetable oil

2 cups thinly sliced red cabbage

1 medium yellow bell pepper, sliced

½ small red onion, sliced

2 garlic cloves, minced

Hoisin sauce, which gives this pork stir-fry savory richness, is a Chinese staple that's sold in most American supermarkets. If you like to create your own stir-fried dishes, there should be a bottle of hoisin sauce in your refrigerator. Made from soybeans, vinegar, garlic, chilies and spices, this sauce can season meat, poultry and shellfish (you can use it in cooking, or as a table condiment). If you buy hoisin sauce in a can, transfer it to a glass jar before you store it.

1 In a medium bowl, combine the hoisin sauce, sherry, soy sauce, honey, cornstarch, sesame oil and red pepper flakes. Stir in the pork and let marinate while you prepare the pasta and vegetables.

2 While the pork is marinating, bring a large covered pot of water to a boil over high heat. Add the spaghettini, return to a boil and cook for 10 to 12 minutes, or according to package directions until al dente. Drain in a colander.

3 While the spaghettini is cooking, in a large no-stick skillet, bring the ⅔ cup of water to a boil over high heat. Add the broccoli florets or broccoli rabe and the carrots, cover and cook for 2 minutes, or until the vegetables are just tender. Drain the vegetables in a colander and transfer to a medium bowl. Wipe the skillet dry.

4 In the dry skillet, warm 1 teaspoon of the oil over medium-high heat. Add the cabbage, bell peppers and onions, and stir-fry for 2 to 3 minutes, or until tender. Add the garlic and stir-fry for 30 seconds, or until fragrant. Transfer to the bowl with the other vegetables.

5 In the skillet, warm the remaining 2 teaspoons oil over medium-high heat. Add the pork and the marinade, and stir-fry for 2 to 3 minutes, or until the pork is cooked through. Add the vegetables and stir-fry for 1 to 2 minutes, or until heated through. Serve over the spaghettini.

Preparation time 25 minutes • **Total time** 35 minutes • **Per serving** 468 calories, 8.8 g. fat (16% of calories), 1.8 g. saturated fat, 33 mg. cholesterol, 557 mg. sodium, 15.8 g. dietary fiber, 155 mg. calcium, 5 mg. iron, 182 mg. vitamin C, 8 mg. beta-carotene • **Serves 4**

SEAFOOD JAMBALAYA

1 tablespoon olive oil

3 ounces baked ham, diced

1 medium green bell pepper, diced

1 medium onion, chopped

2 celery stalks, chopped

3 garlic cloves, minced

1 cup long-grain white rice

1 bay leaf, preferably imported

½ teaspoon dried oregano

½ teaspoon dried thyme

½ teaspoon freshly ground black pepper

¼ teaspoon salt

⅛ teaspoon ground red pepper

1½ cups defatted reduced-sodium chicken broth

1½ cups water

8 ounces sea scallops, tough muscle removed

8 ounces medium shrimp, peeled and deveined, with tails attached

1 cup diced ripe tomatoes

¼ cup chopped Italian parsley

Not many foods have found their way into the lyrics of American popular songs: Jambalaya (and its Cajun companions, crawfish pie and filé gumbo) has that rare distinction. One of the defining dishes of Louisiana cuisine, jambalaya is delightfully variable, subject to the whims of the person cooking it (although the rice, onions, celery and bell peppers are unvarying ingredients). The shrimp-scallop-and-ham jambalaya here is just one interpretation of a dish that is frequently made with sausage, crayfish or oysters.

1 In a large no-stick skillet, warm the oil over medium-high heat. Add the ham, bell peppers, onions, celery and garlic, and sauté for 4 to 5 minutes, or until the vegetables are softened.

2 Stir in the rice, bay leaf, oregano, thyme, black pepper, salt and ground red pepper, and sauté for 1 minute. Add the broth and water, and bring to a boil. Reduce the heat to medium-low, cover and simmer for 15 minutes, or until the rice is just tender.

3 Stir in the scallops, shrimp and tomatoes; cover and simmer for 5 minutes, or until the seafood turns opaque. Just before serving, sprinkle the jambalaya with the chopped parsley.

Preparation time 25 minutes • **Total time** 35 minutes • **Per serving** 383 calories, 7.2 g. fat (17% of calories), 1.5 g. saturated fat, 101 mg. cholesterol, 883 mg. sodium, 2.6 g. dietary fiber, 92 mg. calcium, 5 mg. iron, 38 mg. vitamin C, 0.4 mg. beta-carotene • **Serves 4**

To chop an onion, first cut off the tip and peel the onion. Make a series of parallel cuts toward (but not through) the root end.

Holding the partially sliced onion together, make a second, perpendicular series of cuts, without cutting all the way through.

Still holding the onion together, turn it on its side and cut crosswise: The onion will fall into tiny dice.

FIVE-SPICE CHICKEN WITH VEGETABLES

2 tablespoons reduced-sodium soy sauce

2 garlic cloves, minced

1½ teaspoons five-spice powder

1 teaspoon grated fresh ginger

1 teaspoon dark sesame oil

¼ teaspoon freshly ground black pepper

12 ounces thin-sliced chicken cutlets

⅓ cup defatted reduced-sodium chicken broth

1 tablespoon dry sherry

2 teaspoons cornstarch

⅛ teaspoon crushed red pepper flakes

3 teaspoons vegetable oil

6 ounces orzo pasta

½ pound green beans, trimmed

4 medium carrots, cut into julienne strips

3 cups small cauliflower florets

½ small red onion, thinly sliced

2 tablespoons water

Sliced scallion greens for garnish (optional)

Like pumpkin-pie spice or *fines herbes,* Chinese five-spice powder is a convenient ready-made seasoning blend. It's usually composed of ground anise or fennel seed, star anise, cloves, cinnamon and Szechuan peppercorns. You can find this unique spice blend at Asian markets, and many supermarkets stock it, too.

1 In a medium bowl, combine 2 teaspoons of the soy sauce, the garlic, five-spice powder, ginger, sesame oil and black pepper. Add the chicken and turn to coat. Refrigerate for 15 minutes.

2 Meanwhile, bring a large covered pot of water to a boil over high heat. In a small bowl, whisk together the broth, sherry, cornstarch, red pepper flakes and remaining 1 tablespoon plus 1 teaspoon soy sauce until smooth; set aside.

3 In a large no-stick skillet, warm 1½ teaspoons of the oil over medium-high heat until hot but not smoking. Add the chicken cutlets and cook, turning once, for 4 minutes, or until golden and cooked through. Transfer the chicken to a cutting board and cut into ¼-inch-wide strips.

4 Add the orzo to the boiling water, return to a boil and cook for 8 minutes, or according to package directions until al dente.

5 While the orzo is cooking, in the large skillet, warm the remaining 1½ teaspoons oil over medium-high heat until very hot but not smoking. Add the beans, carrots, cauliflower and onions, and cook, stirring, for 1 minute. Add the water, cover and cook for 2 minutes, or until the vegetables are just tender. Stir in the reserved chicken-broth mixture; reduce the heat to medium-low and simmer for 1 minute. Add the chicken and cook for 30 seconds longer.

6 Drain the orzo and divide it among 4 plates. Top with the chicken and vegetables, and garnish with sliced scallion greens, if desired.

Preparation time 25 minutes • **Total time** 35 minutes • **Per serving** 384 calories, 6.8 g. fat (16% of calories), 1 g. saturated fat, 49 mg. cholesterol, 454 mg. sodium, 6.5 g. dietary fiber, 86 mg. calcium, 4 mg. iron, 72 mg. vitamin C, 12.4 mg. beta-carotene • **Serves 4**

TUSCAN PORK WITH WHITE BEANS

- 1 **pound well-trimmed, lean pork tenderloin**
- ¼ **teaspoon freshly ground black pepper**
- ⅛ **teaspoon salt**
- 1 **tablespoon plus 1 teaspoon olive oil**
- ½ **cup sliced shallots**
- ¼ **teaspoon dried thyme or 1 teaspoon fresh thyme**
- 3 **tablespoons balsamic vinegar**
- 2 **cans (19 ounces each) cannellini beans, rinsed and drained**
- 1 **can (14½ ounces) Italian-style stewed tomatoes with juice**
- ¼ **cup defatted reduced-sodium chicken broth**
- ⅛ **teaspoon crushed red pepper flakes**
- 2 **cups packed fresh spinach leaves or Swiss chard leaves, sliced**

Beans have a long history in Tuscany, stretching back to the 16th century when they were first brought from the New World. White beans—cannellini—are eaten fresh when first picked in June; as the year progresses, the beans become increasingly drier, and cooking times must be adjusted accordingly. Canned beans eliminate any such guesswork from this recipe, in which the beans, bathed in a tart tomato sauce, serve as a foil for tasty pork medallions.

1 Cut the pork tenderloin crosswise into 8 pieces. Place each piece of tenderloin between 2 sheets of wax paper and pound to ½ inch thick. Sprinkle both sides of the pork with the black pepper and salt.

2 In a large no-stick skillet, warm 3 teaspoons of the oil over medium-high heat until very hot but not smoking. Add the pork and cook for 3 minutes per side, or until browned and cooked through. With a slotted spoon, transfer the pork to a plate; cover loosely to keep warm.

3 Add the remaining 1 teaspoon oil to the skillet. Add the shallots and thyme, and sauté for 1 minute. Stir in the vinegar and bring to a boil. Stir in the beans, tomatoes, broth and red pepper flakes, and return to a boil. Reduce the heat to medium-low and simmer for 5 minutes, or until slightly thickened. Stir in the spinach or Swiss chard and simmer for 1 minute, or until the spinach or chard is just wilted.

4 Divide the bean mixture among 4 plates. Top each portion with 2 pork medallions.

Preparation time 20 minutes • **Total time** 35 minutes • **Per serving** 428 calories, 10 g. fat (21% of calories), 2.1 g. saturated fat, 74 mg. cholesterol, 897 mg. sodium, 14.4 g. dietary fiber, 117 mg. calcium, 6 mg. iron, 29 mg. vitamin C, 2 mg. beta-carotene • **Serves 4**

Shallots look like miniature onions. When you remove the outer layer of skin, you'll see that they separate into cloves, like a head of garlic.

ON THE MENU
Make it a totally Tuscan meal: For starters, arrange individual salads of thinly sliced fennel and mushrooms, dressed with an olive-oil and balsamic vinaigrette. Serve whole-wheat Italian bread with the main course; and for a dessert that is quintes-sentially Tuscan, offer biscotti and ripe pears with a dessert wine or espresso.

KITCHEN TIP
Shallots, like garlic cloves, are easier to peel if you first blanch them in boiling water for 1 minute, then rinse them.

SCALLOP SAUTÉ WITH VEGETABLES

¾ **cup raw converted white rice**

1½ **cups water**

1 **pound sea scallops**

1 **tablespoon olive oil**

1 **medium zucchini, halved lengthwise and then cut crosswise into ¼-inch-thick slices**

½ **teaspoon dried basil, crumbled**

⅛ **teaspoon salt**

⅛ **teaspoon freshly ground black pepper**

⅛ **teaspoon crushed red pepper flakes (optional)**

½ **cup diced, drained roasted red peppers (from a jar)**

2 **tablespoons chopped fresh Italian parsley**

Scallops, unlike oysters and clams, really have no season: These succulent morsels, enclosed within fanlike shells, are harvested throughout the year on both the East and West coasts. Sweet, tender scallops are almost always sold shucked; the only preparation they sometimes require is the removal of a small piece of tough connective tissue that may remain after shucking.

1 In a heavy, medium saucepan, combine the rice and water; bring to a boil over high heat. Reduce the heat to low, cover and simmer for 20 minutes, or until the rice is tender and the liquid has been absorbed.

2 Meanwhile, rinse and pat dry the scallops. If any of the scallops are very large, cut them in half crosswise.

3 In a large no-stick skillet, warm the oil over high heat. Add the scallops, zucchini, basil, salt, black pepper and red pepper flakes, if using; sauté the scallops and zucchini for 4 to 5 minutes, or until the scallops are opaque at their thickest part and the zucchini slices are tender. Add the roasted red peppers and sauté for 30 seconds longer, or until the peppers are heated through.

4 Remove the skillet from the heat and stir in the parsley. Spoon the scallop mixture over the hot rice.

Preparation time 10 minutes • **Total time** 30 minutes • **Per serving** 271 calories, 4.6 g. fat (15% of calories), 0.6 g. saturated fat, 38 mg. cholesterol, 260 mg. sodium, 0.7 g. dietary fiber, 54 mg. calcium, 3 mg. iron, 27 mg. vitamin C, 0.6 mg. beta-carotene • **Serves 4**

If some of the scallops you buy have a rubbery piece of connective tissue on one side, just pull it off with your fingers.

FOR A CHANGE
Use yellow summer squash or pattypan squash instead of zucchini. Subtly flavor the rice with garlic by adding a peeled garlic clove to the cooking water. Remove the garlic before serving.

ON THE MENU
This meal is low enough in calories and fat to be a good choice when you want

to splurge on dessert at a family birthday party or other special occasion. Such an extra-light main dish lets you enjoy a slice of cake with a clear conscience.

FOOD FACT
Red pepper flakes are crushed, dried hot chilies; the seeds are included, making this is a very powerful spice—a pinch or two will usually suffice.

SOUTHWESTERN CHICKEN SAUTÉ

1 tablespoon chili powder

1¼ teaspoons ground cumin

¼ teaspoon salt

⅛ teaspoon ground red pepper

1 pound skinless, boneless chicken breast halves (4)

2 teaspoons olive oil

½ cup defatted chicken broth

1 tablespoon cider vinegar

8 ounces ripe plum tomatoes, diced

1 cup frozen corn kernels

1 can (4 ounces) mild green chilies, rinsed and drained

¼ cup chopped fresh cilantro

1 lime, cut into wedges

The chicken is topped with a super-chunky warm "salsa" made with tomatoes, corn and chilies. A quick chili rub gets the chicken off to a flavorful start, and more of the chili mixture goes into the sauce. Chili powder is a spice blend, but ground red pepper is unadulterated "heat": Leave it out if you want a milder dish.

1 In a cup, mix the chili powder, cumin, salt and pepper. Rub both sides of the chicken breasts with 1 tablespoon of the spice mixture.

2 In a large, heavy no-stick skillet, warm the oil over medium-high heat. Add the chicken and sauté for 2 to 3 minutes per side, or until the spice coating is browned and the surface of the chicken is opaque. (The chicken will finish cooking later.) Transfer the chicken to a clean plate.

3 Add the broth, vinegar and the remaining spice mixture to the skillet; increase the heat to high and bring to a boil, stirring to get up the browned bits from the bottom of the skillet. Boil for 1 to 2 minutes, or until the liquid is slightly reduced.

4 Return the chicken to the skillet, adding any juices that have collected on the plate. Add the tomatoes, corn and chilies, and bring to a simmer. Spoon the corn and tomato mixture over the chicken; reduce the heat to medium, cover and simmer, stirring once or twice, for 5 minutes, or until the chicken is cooked through and the flavors are blended. Transfer the chicken and vegetables to a serving dish and sprinkle with the cilantro.

5 Serve the chicken and vegetables with the lime wedges.

Cilantro, or Chinese parsley, looks something like flat-leaf parsley. If you're not sure which is which, crush a leaf between your fingers—the aroma of cilantro is unmistakable.

Preparation time 10 minutes • **Total time** 30 minutes • **Per serving** 214 calories, 4.9 g. fat (20% of calories), 0.7 g. saturated fat, 66 mg. cholesterol, 410 mg. sodium, 2.6 g. dietary fiber, 37 mg. calcium, 2 mg. iron, 21 mg. vitamin C, 0.7 mg. beta-carotene • **Serves 4**

ON THE MENU
The perfect partner for the chicken and vegetables is a corn or flour tortilla or a slice of cornbread. And serve a salad of chilled blanched green beans and ripe tomato wedges with a vinaigrette dressing.

PART 3
Poultry Dishes

ROSEMARY-ORANGE CHICKEN ON SPINACH

1 large navel orange

2–3 tablespoons orange juice

1 tablespoon olive oil

2 teaspoons balsamic vinegar

½ teaspoon dried rosemary, crumbled

¼ teaspoon light brown sugar

Pinch of crushed red pepper flakes

1 pound thin-sliced chicken cutlets

¼ teaspoon freshly ground black pepper

¼ teaspoon salt

1 pound washed spinach, tough stems removed

The novel interplay of seasonings in this dish will surprise and intrigue anyone who ever thought chicken was boring: There's the freshness of citrus, the mellow tang of balsamic vinegar, the pungency of rosemary and the bite of black and red pepper. If you can't find balsamic vinegar, which is carefully aged to produce its unique flavor, substitute a mild red wine vinegar.

1 Grate ½ teaspoon of zest from the orange; set the zest aside. Using a sharp paring knife, peel the orange, removing all of the white pith. Working over a bowl, cut between the membranes to divide the orange into sections. Squeeze the membranes between your fingers to release all the juice, then discard them. Pour all the juice from the bowl into a measuring cup, then add enough additional orange juice to measure ⅓ cup.

2 Add the orange zest, 1 teaspoon of the oil, the vinegar, ¼ teaspoon of the rosemary, the sugar and red pepper flakes to the orange juice, and whisk until blended; set aside.

3 Sprinkle the chicken with the remaining ¼ teaspoon rosemary, the black pepper and salt. In a large no-stick skillet, warm the remaining 2 teaspoons oil over high heat until hot but not smoking. Working in batches, if necessary, add the chicken and sauté for 2 to 3 minutes per side, or until lightly browned and cooked through. Transfer the chicken to a platter and cover loosely with a sheet of foil.

4 Add the spinach to the skillet and stir-fry over high heat for 1 to 2 minutes, or just until the spinach is wilted.

5 Arrange the spinach around the chicken on the platter and place the orange sections on the chicken.

6 Whisk the dressing briefly to reblend it, then pour the dressing over the chicken and spinach.

Preparation time 25 minutes • **Total time** 35 minutes • **Per serving** 199 calories, 5.1 g. fat (23% of calories), 1 g. saturated fat, 66 mg. cholesterol, 274 mg. sodium, 3.2 g. dietary fiber, 115 mg. calcium, 3 mg. iron, 54 mg. vitamin C, 3.4 mg. beta-carotene • **Serves 4**

Turkey Tonkatsu with Vegetables

1 teaspoon vegetable oil

1 large egg white

3 tablespoons water

½ cup unseasoned dry bread crumbs

1 tablespoon plus ½ teaspoon grated fresh ginger

1 tablespoon reduced-sodium soy sauce

1 pound thin-sliced turkey breast cutlets (4)

3 cups cauliflower florets

2 cups thinly sliced carrots

3 tablespoons rice vinegar

1 tablespoon honey

¼ teaspoon salt

¼ teaspoon crushed red pepper flakes

¼ teaspoon freshly ground black pepper

2 scallions, thinly sliced on the diagonal

2 teaspoons dark sesame oil

Tonkatsu means "pork cutlet," but this turkey variation is lighter than the original. The crumbed cutlets are usually fried in oil; baking them in the oven cuts lots of fat from the dish. The pickled vegetables are *sunomono*—Japanese for "vinegared things."

1 Brush a jelly-roll pan with the vegetable oil.

2 In a shallow bowl, using a fork, beat the egg white and 1 tablespoon of the water until frothy. Place the bread crumbs on a plate.

3 On another plate, mix 1½ teaspoons of the ginger with the soy sauce. Dip both sides of each turkey cutlet into the soy-sauce mixture. Dip the cutlets into the egg white, let the excess drip off, then dredge in the bread crumbs, pressing the crumbs into the surface. Arrange the turkey in a single layer in the prepared pan. Cover with a sheet of wax paper and set aside.

4 Preheat the oven to 425°.

5 In a medium saucepan, bring 1 inch of water to a boil over high heat. Add the cauliflower and carrots, and return to a boil. Cook for 4 to 6 minutes, or until the vegetables are crisp-tender. Drain in a colander and transfer to a serving bowl.

6 In the same saucepan, combine the remaining 2 teaspoons ginger, the vinegar, honey, salt, red pepper flakes, black pepper and remaining 2 tablespoons water, and bring to a boil over high heat, stirring.

7 Add half the scallions to the bowl of vegetables, then pour on the hot dressing and toss to mix; place the bowl in the freezer to chill.

8 Drizzle the sesame oil over the turkey and bake for 5 minutes. Turn and bake for 5 minutes longer, or until browned, crisp and cooked through. Cut the turkey diagonally into strips. Garnish the pickled vegetables with the remaining scallions and serve with the turkey.

Preparation time 15 minutes • **Total time** 30 minutes • **Per serving** 280 calories, 5.1 g. fat (16% of calories), 0.9 g. saturated fat, 70 mg. cholesterol, 505 mg. sodium, 4.3 g. dietary fiber, 88 mg. calcium, 3 mg. iron, 60 mg. vitamin C, 0.9 mg. beta-carotene • **Serves 4**

❧   ❧   ❧

CRISPY CHICKEN WITH NECTARINE SALSA

1 large egg white

2 tablespoons plus 1 teaspoon fresh lime juice

½ cup unseasoned dry bread crumbs

1½ teaspoons chili powder

1¼ teaspoons ground cumin

¼ teaspoon salt

1 pound skinless, boneless chicken breast halves (4)

12 ounces ripe nectarines, diced

½ cup finely diced red bell peppers

2 tablespoons chopped fresh cilantro

1 tablespoon minced red onion

1 tablespoon honey

½ teaspoon minced, seeded pickled jalapeño pepper

⅛ teaspoon freshly ground black pepper

2 teaspoons olive oil

Peruse the menus of the country's trendiest restaurants and you'll find salsas made with pineapples, mangoes, cranberries, bananas, and just about any other fruit you can think of. This sweet-hot nectarine-and-jalapeño salsa is the ideal companion for crisp-crusted chicken breasts.

1 Spray a jelly-roll pan with no-stick spray.

2 In a shallow bowl or pie plate, using a fork, lightly beat the egg white with 1 tablespoon of the lime juice until frothy. In another shallow bowl, mix the bread crumbs, chili powder, 1 teaspoon of the cumin and the salt. One at a time, dip the chicken breasts into the egg white, letting the excess drip off, then roll the chicken in the crumbs, pressing them into the surface. Place the chicken breasts, skinned-side up, on the prepared pan. Set the chicken aside, uncovered.

3 Preheat the oven to 450°.

4 In a medium bowl, combine the nectarines, bell peppers, cilantro, onions, honey, jalapeño, black pepper, the remaining 1 tablespoon plus 1 teaspoon lime juice and remaining ¼ teaspoon cumin. Cover and set aside.

5 Drizzle the chicken evenly with the oil and bake for 10 minutes. Turn the chicken and bake for 5 minutes longer, or until crisp, lightly browned, and cooked through.

6 Serve the chicken with the nectarine salsa.

Preparation time 20 minutes • **Total time** 35 minutes • **Per serving** 257 calories, 5.1 g. fat (18% of calories), 0.8 g. saturated fat, 66 mg. cholesterol, 283 mg. sodium, 2.3 g. dietary fiber, 51 mg. calcium, 2 mg. iron, 32 mg. vitamin C, 1 mg. beta-carotene
Serves 4

SUBSTITUTION
Use peaches if nectarines are not available. Or substitute unsweetened frozen peach slices when the fresh fruits are out of season.

FOOD FACT
Nectarines and peaches are closely related, and the two fruits have been cross-bred to produce sweetier, tastier peaches and bigger nectarines.

LEMON-ROSEMARY CHICKEN BREASTS

2 large lemons

2 tablespoons packed light brown sugar

1½ teaspoons coarsely chopped fresh rosemary leaves or ½ teaspoon dried

¼ teaspoon salt

¼ teaspoon freshly ground black pepper

2 pounds skinless bone-in chicken breast halves (4)

1 teaspoon cornstarch dissolved in 1 tablespoon cold water

Fresh rosemary sprigs for garnish (optional)

Here's a quick dinner that you can put together even when there's no time to shop. You can keep all the ingredients on hand, including the rosemary, which will last in the refrigerator for up to ten days. Of course, you can use dried rosemary instead of fresh. If you're substituting the dried herb, crumble it between your fingers to release its fragrance.

1 Preheat the oven to 400°. Spray a 9 x 13-inch baking pan with no-stick spray.

2 Grate 2 teaspoons of zest from one lemon, then halve the lemon and squeeze 3 tablespoons of juice from it into a shallow medium bowl. Cut the other lemon into thin slices, discarding the ends.

3 Add the lemon zest, sugar, rosemary, salt and pepper to the bowl of lemon juice and whisk to blend. One at time, dip the chicken breasts into the lemon mixture, turning to coat both sides.

4 Arrange the chicken breasts, skinned side up, in the prepared pan and place some of the lemon slices on top of each. (If any of the lemon mixture remains in the bowl, spoon it over the chicken.) Bake, basting twice with the pan juices, for 25 to 30 minutes, or until the chicken is cooked through.

5 Transfer the chicken to plates. Pour the pan juices into a small saucepan, stir in the cornstarch mixture and bring to a boil over medium heat, stirring constantly until thickened. Spoon the pan juices over the chicken. Garnish with rosemary sprigs, if desired.

Preparation time 5 minutes • **Total time** 35 minutes • **Per serving** 232 calories, 2.5 g. fat (10% of calories), 1 g. saturated fat, 101 mg. cholesterol, 253 mg. sodium, 0 g. dietary fiber, 47 mg. calcium, 2 mg. iron, 30 mg. vitamin C, 0 mg. beta-carotene
Serves 4

KITCHEN TIPS
Wrap fresh rosemary in a small plastic bag and store it in the crisper drawer of the refrigerator.

ON THE MENU
Steamed green beans or yellow wax beans (or a mix of the two) and crisp rolls make this meal complete.

TURKEY CUTLETS MILANESE

- 1 large egg white
- 1 tablespoon water
- ½ cup unseasoned dry bread crumbs
- ½ teaspoon freshly ground black pepper
- ¼ teaspoon dried oregano, crumbled
- 1 pound thinly sliced turkey breast cutlets (4)
- 2 tablespoons defatted chicken broth
- 1 tablespoon plus 1 teaspoon extra-virgin olive oil
- 2 teaspoons red wine vinegar
- 1 small garlic clove, crushed through a press
- 1 teaspoon Dijon mustard
- ⅛ teaspoon salt
- 4 firmly packed cups (2 large bunches) arugula, watercress or spinach, washed and trimmed
- 1 large fresh tomato (about 10 ounces), cut into large dice
- ½ cup thinly sliced radishes
- ¼ cup thinly sliced sweet red or white onion
- ½ ounce Parmesan cheese, shaved with a vegetable peeler (about 2 tablespoons)

Egg-dipped, crumbed and gently sautéed in butter, thinly sliced veal *alla Milanese* turns out juicy and tender despite the delicacy of the meat. Thin turkey breast cutlets are a fine substitute for veal; baked with just a drizzling of olive oil, they emerge crisp-crusted and delicious. The somewhat sharp-flavored salad of greens, radishes, onions and Parmesan provides a refreshing contrast.

1 Preheat the oven to 450°. Spray a jelly-roll pan with no-stick spray.

2 In a shallow bowl or pie plate, using a fork, beat the egg white and water until frothy. In another shallow bowl, or on a sheet of wax paper, combine the bread crumbs, ¼ teaspoon of the pepper and the oregano.

3 One at time, dip the turkey cutlets into the egg mixture, letting the excess drip off, then coat with the crumbs, pressing them into the surface. Arrange the cutlets in a single layer in the prepared pan and let stand while you prepare the salad dressing.

4 In a medium bowl, whisk together the broth, 2 teaspoons of the oil, the vinegar, garlic, mustard, salt and the remaining ¼ teaspoon pepper; set aside.

5 Drizzle the turkey with the remaining 2 teaspoons oil and bake, turning once, for 6 to 8 minutes, or until lightly browned and cooked through.

6 Arrange the turkey cutlets on a heated platter. Add the arugula or other greens, the tomatoes, radishes and onions to the dressing, and toss to coat. Spoon the salad over the cutlets. Sprinkle with the Parmesan and serve.

Preparation time 20 minutes • **Total time** 30 minutes • **Per serving** 273 calories, 7.9 g. fat (26% of calories), 1.8 g. saturated fat, 73 mg. cholesterol, 421 mg. sodium, 3.2 g. dietary fiber, 166 mg. calcium, 3 mg. iron, 40 mg. vitamin C, 1.7 mg. beta-carotene • **Serves 4**

KITCHEN TIPS
If you're using arugula or spinach for the salad, tear any large leaves into pieces.

Use a vegetable peeler to pare shavings from a piece of Parmesan. This is easier to do if the cheese is at room temperature.

TURKEY-SAGE CUTLETS WITH MUSHROOMS

⅓ cup dried mushrooms, preferably porcini (¼ ounce)

1 cup boiling water

1 pound thin-sliced turkey cutlets (4 cutlets)

¼ teaspoon salt

¼ teaspoon freshly ground black pepper

1½ teaspoons grated lemon zest

4 large fresh sage leaves plus ½ teaspoon coarsely chopped fresh sage

1 tablespoon all-purpose flour

1 tablespoon grated Parmesan cheese

1 tablespoon plus 1 teaspoon olive oil

12 ounces white button mushrooms, sliced

3 tablespoons dry Marsala

Marsala, a fortified wine produced in western Sicily, gives this dish a light winy "bouquet." If you prefer, substitute 4 teaspoons of grape juice plus 4 teaspoons of beef broth.

1 Place the dried mushrooms in a large heatproof measuring cup and pour the boiling water over them; let stand for 10 to 15 minutes, or until softened. Meanwhile, line a small strainer with cheesecloth.

2 With a slotted spoon, transfer the mushrooms from the soaking liquid to a cutting board and chop. Place the strainer over a small bowl and pour the soaking liquid through it, leaving the sediment in the cup. Reserve about ¼ cup of the soaking liquid.

3 Season the cutlets with the salt and black pepper. Rub one side of each cutlet with the lemon zest. Place a sage leaf on the bottom half of the zested side of each cutlet, then fold the cutlets in half crosswise. In a small bowl, combine the flour and Parmesan; dust the cutlets with the mixture.

4 In a large no-stick skillet, warm 2 teaspoons of the oil over medium-high heat. Sauté the cutlets, turning once halfway through cooking, for 6 to 8 minutes, or until browned and cooked through. Transfer the cutlets to a platter and cover loosely to keep warm.

5 Add the remaining 2 teaspoons oil to the skillet and warm over medium-high heat. Add the fresh mushrooms and softened dried mushrooms, and sauté for 2 minutes. Drizzle with 2 tablespoons of the reserved soaking liquid and the Marsala. Sauté for 2 to 3 minutes, or until the mushrooms are tender and the liquid is absorbed. Add a little more soaking liquid if the pan gets too dry. Pour any juices from the platter over the mushrooms, sprinkle with the chopped sage and simmer for 30 seconds.

6 Serve the cutlets topped with the mushrooms.

Preparation time 10 minutes • **Total time** 30 minutes • **Per serving** 220 calories, 6 g. fat (24% of calories), 1.1 g. saturated fat, 71 mg. cholesterol, 219 mg. sodium, 1.2 g. dietary fiber, 40 mg. calcium, 3 mg. iron, 4 mg. vitamin C, 0 mg. beta-carotene
Serves 4

CHICKEN BREASTS WITH PEARS

½ teaspoon dried thyme, crumbled

¼ teaspoon salt

¼ teaspoon freshly ground black pepper

1 pound skinless, boneless chicken breast halves (4)

2 teaspoons olive oil

½ cup pear nectar

¼ cup defatted chicken broth

2 teaspoons balsamic vinegar

2 teaspoons honey

2 large ripe pears (about 1 pound), cut into ½-inch dice

1 teaspoon cornstarch dissolved in 1 tablespoon defatted chicken broth or cold water

1 teaspoon unsalted butter or margarine

½ ounce toasted coarsely chopped walnuts

The technique used to create this dish is one you can use again and again for quick meals: The chicken breasts are sautéed in a skillet and removed, then a sauce is made in the same skillet, using a few simple ingredients. It's a one-pot meal that can be casual or celebratory, depending on the sauce and side dishes.

1 In a cup, mix the thyme, salt and pepper. Season the chicken on both sides with the herb mixture.

2 In a large, heavy no-stick skillet, warm the oil over medium-high heat. Add the chicken and sauté for 4 to 6 minutes per side, or until cooked through, reducing the heat slightly if necessary. Transfer to a large platter and cover loosely with foil to keep warm.

3 Add the pear nectar, broth, vinegar and honey to the skillet, and bring to a boil over medium-high heat, stirring frequently.

4 Add the pears to the skillet, bring to a boil and reduce the heat to medium-low. Cover and simmer, stirring occasionally, for 2 to 3 minutes, or until the pears are tender. Pour any juices that have collected on the chicken platter into the skillet. Stir in the cornstarch mixture, then the butter or margarine; return the sauce to a boil, stirring gently until slightly thickened. Remove the skillet from the heat.

5 Transfer the chicken to plates; spoon the pears and sauce over the chicken. Sprinkle with the walnuts.

Preparation time 10 minutes • **Total time** 30 minutes • **Per serving** 272 calories, 7.3 g. fat (24% of calories), 1.5 g. saturated fat, 68 mg. cholesterol, 273 mg. sodium, 3.1 g. dietary fiber, 35 mg. calcium, 2 mg. iron, 6 mg. vitamin C, 0 mg. beta-carotene
Serves 4

ON THE MENU
Accompany the chicken with sautéed kale and a mixture of brown and wild rice.

SUBSTITUTION
If pear nectar isn't available, you can substitute apple cider.

FOOD FACT
We owe the development of many modern pear varieties to the French nobility of the 17th, 18th and 19th centuries. Gentlemen cultivated pears as a hobby, and they perfected, among others, the Anjou, Comice and what we now call the Bartlett pear.

CHICKEN PICCATA WITH ESCAROLE

12 ounces skinless, boneless chicken breast halves (4)

½ teaspoon dried thyme, crumbled

¼ teaspoon freshly ground black pepper

1½ teaspoons olive oil

2 garlic cloves, minced

5 cups loosely packed cut-up escarole

1 cup halved cherry tomatoes

⅛ teaspoon salt

2 teaspoons cornstarch dissolved in ½ cup defatted chicken broth

½ teaspoon grated lemon zest

1 tablespoon fresh lemon juice

1 teaspoon unsalted butter or margarine

Although it is frequently served as a salad green, escarole is also delicious sautéed with garlic and served warm.

Classic sauces start out rich: Cream, butter and eggs are the basic of many of them. Beyond that, there's a technique called "enrichment," in which more of these luxurious ingredients are added after the sauce is made. Egg yolks and cream may be beaten in, or additional butter whisked into the sauce. Taking a tip from the great chefs, you can also enrich a light sauce like this one; one teaspoon of butter adds just a gram of fat per serving but makes a notable difference in the flavor.

1 Preheat the broiler and a broiler-pan rack.

2 Season both sides of the chicken breasts with the thyme and pepper. Place the chicken on the broiler-pan rack and broil 2 to 3 inches from the heat for about 5 minutes per side, or until it is browned and cooked through. Transfer the chicken to a warm platter and cover it loosely with foil.

3 Meanwhile, in a large, deep skillet, warm the oil over medium-high heat. Add the garlic and sauté, stirring constantly, for 30 seconds, or until fragrant. Add the escarole, increase the heat to high and sauté, tossing frequently, for 2 to 3 minutes, or until the greens begin to wilt. Add the cherry tomatoes and cook for 2 to 3 minutes, or until the tomatoes are warm and soft and the escarole is completely wilted. Add the salt, then transfer the vegetables to the warm platter.

4 In the same skillet, whisk together the cornstarch mixture, lemon zest and lemon juice, and bring to a boil over high heat, stirring constantly. Simmer, stirring, for 1 to 2 minutes, or until the sauce is slightly thickened and bubbly. Add the butter or margarine and any juices that have collected on the platter, and return to a boil, stirring. Cook just until the butter or margarine is melted and the sauce has thickened. Pour the sauce over the chicken and vegetables.

Preparation time 10 minutes • **Total time** 30 minutes • **Per serving** 148 calories, 4.1 g. fat (25% of calories), 1.1 g. saturated fat, 52 mg. cholesterol, 268 mg. sodium, 2.1 g. dietary fiber, 60 mg. calcium, 2 mg. iron, 13 mg. vitamin C, 1 mg. beta-carotene
Serves 4

CHICKEN MOZZARELLA

6 ounces ditalini pasta or other small macaroni

½ teaspoon dried thyme

½ teaspoon dried basil

⅛ teaspoon salt

⅛ teaspoon garlic powder

⅛ teaspoon crushed red pepper flakes

8 ounces thin-sliced chicken breast cutlets, cut into strips

1 teaspoon olive oil

2½ cups halved cherry tomatoes

1 medium zucchini (about 8 ounces), halved lengthwise and thinly sliced

1 cup coarsely diced red onion

¼ cup defatted chicken broth

¼ cup water

1 can (10 ounces) red kidney beans, rinsed and drained

3 ounces shredded part-skim mozzarella cheese

1 tablespoon chopped fresh Italian parsley (optional)

When the word "cheese"—or the name of a specific cheese—is in a recipe title, it's usually a good bet that the dish is loaded with fat. At a restaurant, you'd want to skip anything labeled "Parmigiana," "Mozzarella" or "Con Quattro Formaggi" (with four cheeses). This chicken-and-pasta combination breaks the rule, with less than seven grams of fat per serving.

1 Bring a covered medium pot of water to a boil over high heat. Add the pasta, return to a boil and cook for 5 to 8 minutes, or according to package directions until al dente. Drain in a colander and set aside.

2 While the pasta is cooking, in a cup, crumble together ¼ teaspoon of the thyme and ¼ teaspoon of the basil with the salt, garlic powder and red pepper flakes. Sprinkle the seasonings over both sides of the chicken strips.

3 Brush a large, heavy no-stick skillet with the oil and heat over medium-high heat. Add the chicken strips and sauté for about 2 minutes per side, or until lightly browned and cooked through. Transfer the cooked chicken to a clean plate.

4 Add the tomatoes, zucchini, onions, broth, water and the remaining ¼ teaspoon thyme and ¼ teaspoon basil to the skillet, and toss to blend well. Simmer, tossing frequently, for 4 to 5 minutes, or until the tomatoes have collapsed and the vegetables are tender. Add the beans and simmer for 2 to 3 minutes, or until heated through. Stir in the drained pasta.

5 Place the chicken on top of the pasta and vegetables; pour any chicken juices that have collected on the plate over the chicken and sprinkle with the cheese. Remove from the heat, cover and let stand for 3 to 4 minutes, or until the cheese is melted. Sprinkle with the parsley, if desired.

Preparation time 10 minutes • **Total time** 30 minutes • **Per serving** 375 calories, 6.7 g. fat (16% of calories), 2.6 g. saturated fat, 45 mg. cholesterol, 370 mg. sodium, 5.6 g. dietary fiber, 199 mg. calcium, 4 mg. iron, 23 mg. vitamin C, 0.4 mg. beta-carotene • **Serves 4**

CHICKEN WITH GINGER-MUSTARD SAUCE

1 **pound thin-sliced chicken breast cutlets**

½ **teaspoon freshly ground black pepper**

¼ **teaspoon ground ginger**

⅛ **teaspoon salt**

2½ **teaspoons extra-virgin olive oil**

½ **cup defatted chicken broth**

1½ **teaspoons cornstarch, dissolved in ¼ cup cold water**

2 **teaspoons grated fresh ginger**

2 **teaspoons coarse Dijon mustard**

¼ **teaspoon dry mustard**

3 **tablespoons light sour cream**

As you whisk the cornstarch mixture into the skillet, the sauce will thicken and become glossy.

There's more than one way to make a cream sauce, as every health- and flavor-conscious cook should know. One French recipe for mustard sauce calls for 1½ cups of heavy cream and a few tablespoons of butter, plus the pan juices from roasted pork that has been basted with butter and lard. In a simple but significant transformation, this ginger-mustard sauce is made in the skillet after you sauté skinless chicken in just 2½ teaspoons of oil; the cornstarch and the prepared and dry mustards thicken the sauce, with light sour cream as a last-minute enrichment.

1 Season the chicken on both sides with the pepper, ground ginger and salt.

2 In a large, heavy no-stick skillet, warm the oil over medium-high heat. Add the chicken and sauté for 2 to 3 minutes per side, or just until browned and cooked through. Transfer the chicken to a platter and cover loosely with foil to keep warm.

3 Whisk the broth, cornstarch mixture, fresh ginger, Dijon mustard and dry mustard into the skillet. Place over medium-high heat and bring to a boil, whisking constantly until the sauce thickens. Remove the skillet from the heat.

4 Pour any chicken juices that have collected on the platter into the sauce and whisk in the sour cream. Spoon the sauce over the chicken.

Preparation time 10 minutes • **Total time** 25 minutes • **Per serving** 181 calories, 6.2 g. fat (31% of calories), 1.5 g. saturated fat, 70 mg. cholesterol, 342 mg. sodium, 0 g. dietary fiber, 16 mg. calcium, 1 mg. iron, 1 mg. vitamin C, 0 mg. beta-carotene
Serves 4

KITCHEN TIPS

Cornstarch, a superfine flour made from the endosperm of the corn kernel, can thicken sauces without adding fat. Here are a few points to remember when cooking with cornstarch. If you stir the starch directly into hot liquid, it will almost certainly form lumps. To prevent this, combine the cornstarch with cold liquid (such as the water used here) and then add the mixture to the hot (not boiling) liquid. Whisk or stir constantly but gently as the cornstarch mixture is added and afterward: Too-vigorous beating—or too-high heat—will defeat the thickening power of the cornstarch.

SAUTÉED CHICKEN WITH PLUMS

1 teaspoon grated lemon zest

½ teaspoon dried thyme, crumbled

¼ teaspoon salt

¼ teaspoon freshly ground
black pepper

⅛ teaspoon ground nutmeg

1 pound skinless, boneless
chicken breast halves (4)

1 tablespoon olive oil

12 ounces ripe plums, cut into
½-inch wedges

⅓ cup apple juice

⅓ cup defatted chicken broth

3 tablespoons plum jam

1 teaspoon fresh lemon juice

2 teaspoons cornstarch, dissolved
in 1 tablespoon cold water

Fresh thyme sprigs for garnish
(optional)

Different varieties of plums will subtly alter the taste of this sauté: Santa Rosas and Casselmans are on the tart side, while Tragedy and Queen Ann plums are sweeter. Be careful not to overcook the plums; the time required will depend on their type and ripeness.

1 In a cup, mix the lemon zest, thyme, salt, pepper and nutmeg. Sprinkle the mixture over both sides of the chicken.

2 In a large, heavy no-stick skillet, warm the oil over medium-high heat. Add the chicken, skinned side down, and reduce the heat to medium. Sauté for 4 to 6 minutes per side, or until cooked through. Transfer the chicken to a clean plate and cover loosely with foil to keep warm.

3 Add the plums to the skillet and sauté for 1 minute, or until they start to soften. Add the apple juice, broth, jam and lemon juice, and bring to a boil. Reduce the heat to medium-low, cover the skillet and simmer, stirring occasionally, for 2 to 3 minutes, or until the plums have softened; be careful not to let them turn mushy.

4 Pour any chicken juices that have collected on the plate into the skillet and then stir in the cornstarch mixture. Increase the heat to medium and cook, stirring constantly but gently to keep the plums intact, until the mixture comes to a boil and thickens. Remove the skillet from the heat.

5 Place the chicken breasts on dinner plates. Spoon the plums and sauce over the chicken and garnish with thyme sprigs, if desired.

Preparation time 12 minutes • **Total time** 30 minutes • **Per serving** 254 calories, 5.5 g. fat (19% of calories), 0.9 g. saturated fat, 66 mg. cholesterol, 297 mg. sodium, 1.9 g. dietary fiber, 27 mg. calcium, 1.3 mg. iron, 20 mg. vitamin C, 0.2 mg. beta-carotene • **Serves 4**

ON THE MENU
Serve the chicken with couscous or rice, topped with a little of the plum sauce.

Carrot sticks or sliced yellow summer squash or zucchini, simply steamed, make a colorful complement to the chicken.

TURKEY WITH CRANBERRY-ORANGE SAUCE

¾ teaspoon dried sage, crumbled

¾ teaspoon coarsely cracked black pepper

¼ teaspoon salt

1 pound thin-sliced turkey breast cutlets (4)

2 cups fresh or frozen cranberries

½ medium navel orange, scrubbed (but not peeled) and cut into small dice

¼ cup water

¼ cup no-sugar-added orange marmalade

2 tablespoons frozen orange juice concentrate

1 tablespoon granulated sugar

⅛ teaspoon ground cinnamon

1 tablespoon olive oil

With a wide variety of ready-to-cook turkey parts available at most supermarkets, this low-fat meat has become tremendously popular. You can choose from drumsticks, wings or thighs, boneless or bone-in breasts, breast cutlets (slices) and tenderloins (fillets). Thin-sliced cutlets are the quickest to cook.

1 In a cup, mix the sage, pepper and salt. Sprinkle both sides of the turkey cutlets with this mixture; cover and set aside.

2 In a heavy medium saucepan, stir together the cranberries, diced orange, water, marmalade, orange juice concentrate, sugar and cinnamon. Bring to a boil over high heat, stirring frequently. Reduce the heat to medium-low, cover and simmer for 4 minutes.

3 Uncover the pot and simmer, stirring occasionally, for 3 to 4 minutes longer, or until the cranberries have popped and softened and the sauce is thickened. Remove from the heat and cover to keep warm.

4 In a large no-stick skillet, warm the oil over high heat. Add the turkey, in batches, and sauté for 1½ to 3 minutes per side, or until browned and cooked through. Serve the turkey with the cranberry sauce.

Preparation time 10 minutes • **Total time** 30 minutes • **Per serving** 261 calories, 4.3 g. fat (15% of calories), 0.7 g. saturated fat, 70 mg. cholesterol, 192 mg. sodium, 0.6 g. dietary fiber, 31 mg. calcium, 2 mg. iron, 30 mg. vitamin C, 0 mg. beta-carotene
Serves 4

To crush peppercorns, spread them on a cutting board; lay the flat of a broad knife blade on them and rap it sharply with the heel of your hand.

MARKET AND PANTRY
Stock up on cranberries when they are most available—in the fall through the winter holidays. Cranberries keep for about a month in the refrigerator, and for up to a year in the freezer, in the unopened bag. Because the berries are dry packed, they pour readily from the bag when frozen; it's not necessary to thaw them before cooking. If you use a standard recipe for cranberry sauce (such as the one on the bag), you can reduce the sugar considerably and still have a tasty sauce. The sauce can also be sweetened with frozen fruit juice concentrates or with the addition of fruits such as pears or raisins.

HEAD START
Make the cranberry sauce ahead of time and serve it either warm or cold. If you like, make a double batch so you have some extra to serve at other meals.

PART 4
Pasta Dishes

BOW-TIES WITH CURRIED BEEF

1 cup plain nonfat yogurt

8 ounces lean, trimmed boneless beef sirloin or top round steak

2 garlic cloves, crushed

1½ teaspoons curry powder

1½ teaspoons ground cumin

6 ounces bow-tie pasta

⅓ cup defatted chicken broth

¼ cup water

1½ cups small cauliflower florets

1½ cups snow peas

¼ cup chopped fresh cilantro

¼ teaspoon salt

Pinch of ground red pepper

Yogurt-cheese funnels are made of fine plastic mesh. Stand the funnel over a bowl or cup and spoon in the yogurt; place in the refrigerator until the yogurt is as thick as you like.

Yogurt, when briefly drained, gets as thick as sour cream, providing a low-fat base for creamy sauces. If you use drained yogurt often (it can substitute for heavy cream or cream cheese, too), buy an inexpensive yogurt funnel like the one shown.

1 Line a coffee-filter cone with a paper filter (or line a small strainer with a white paper towel) and place over a small bowl. Spoon the yogurt into the filter or strainer and let drain for 15 minutes.

2 While the yogurt drains, bring a large covered pot of water to a boil over high heat. Meanwhile, preheat the broiler and the broiler pan and rack. Rub the steak with the garlic, ½ teaspoon of the curry powder and ½ teaspoon of the cumin. Let stand for 5 minutes.

3 Place the steak on the broiler-pan rack and broil 4 to 6 inches from the heat source for 5 minutes per side, or until medium-rare. Transfer to a plate and let stand for 5 minutes.

4 While the steak broils, add the pasta to the boiling water, return to a boil and cook for 10 to 12 minutes or according to package directions until al dente. Drain in a colander and transfer to a serving bowl.

5 In a medium skillet, bring the broth and water to a boil over high heat. Add the cauliflower, reduce the heat to medium-high, cover and cook for 3 to 4 minutes, or until crisp-tender. Uncover the pan, stir in the snow peas and cook for 1 to 2 minutes longer, or until crisp-tender. Pour the vegetable mixture over the pasta.

6 Mix the drained yogurt with the cilantro, the remaining 1 teaspoon curry powder, remaining 1 teaspoon cumin and the salt and red pepper. Add the yogurt mixture to the pasta and toss to coat.

7 Transfer the steak to a cutting board; pour any juices from the plate over the pasta. Thinly slice the steak, add it to the pasta and toss.

Preparation time 10 minutes • **Total time** 35 minutes • **Per serving** 314 calories, 4.4 g. fat (12% of calories), 1.4 g. saturated fat, 39 mg. cholesterol, 301 mg. sodium, 3.6 g. dietary fiber, 175 mg. calcium, 5 mg. iron, 60 mg. vitamin C, 0.1 mg. beta-carotene • **Serves 4**

TORTELLONI WITH VEGETABLE SAUCE

2 cans (14½ ounces each) no-salt-added stewed tomatoes with their juice

2 tablespoons no-salt-added tomato paste

1 medium zucchini, thinly sliced

1 medium yellow squash, thinly sliced

2 garlic cloves, crushed

2 teaspoons dried Italian herb seasoning

12 ounces fresh or frozen meat tortelloni

2 teaspoons cornstarch

2 tablespoons grated Parmesan cheese

¼ cup chopped fresh basil, or 2 tablespoons chopped Italian parsley

Filled pastas such as tortelloni and the smaller tortellini are sold both fresh and frozen in many supermarkets. They are almost a meal in themselves, requiring just a simple sauce and a salad to make a well-balanced dinner. This sauce, made with tomatoes and summer squash, can also be served over unfilled pasta such as rotelle.

1 Bring a large covered pot of water to a boil over high heat.

2 Meanwhile, in a cup, set aside 1 tablespoon of the juice from the stewed tomatoes. In a large, heavy saucepan, stir together the stewed tomatoes with their remaining juice and the tomato paste. Stir in the zucchini, yellow squash, garlic and Italian seasoning; cover and bring to a boil over medium-high heat. Reduce the heat to low; simmer, stirring occasionally, for 5 minutes, or until the vegetables are tender.

3 Add the pasta to the boiling water, return to a boil and cook for 8 to 10 minutes or according to package directions until al dente. Drain the pasta in a colander and transfer to a warmed serving bowl.

4 Stir the cornstarch into the reserved tomato juice. Stir the cornstarch mixture and the Parmesan into the vegetable sauce and bring to a boil, stirring constantly; the sauce will thicken slightly. Remove the pan from the heat and stir in the basil or parsley.

5 Pour the vegetable sauce over the pasta and serve.

Preparation time 11 minutes • **Total time** 25 minutes • **Per serving** 355 calories, 5.4 g. fat (14% of calories), 0.7 g. saturated fat, 52 mg. cholesterol, 496 mg. sodium, 5.8 g. dietary fiber, 224 mg. calcium, 5 mg. iron, 40 mg. vitamin C, 1.1 mg. beta-carotene • **Serves 4**

ON THE MENU
Try an Italian salad of thinly sliced fennel, sliced mushrooms (either nut-brown cremini or white button mushrooms) and shavings of Parmesan, lightly dressed with a lemon vinaigrette.

FOR A CHANGE
There are lots of stuffed pastas, with a variety of fillings, to sample: *cappelletti* (little hats), the filled pasta crescents called *agnolotti* and triangular *pansotti* as well as the more familiar tortellini and ravioli.

PENNE AND STEAK SALAD

½ cup (1 ounce) sun-dried tomatoes (not packed in oil)

1 cup water

6 ounces penne pasta

8 ounces lean, trimmed boneless beef sirloin or top round steak

2 garlic cloves, crushed

½ teaspoon coarsely cracked black pepper

2 tablespoons defatted beef broth

1 tablespoon fresh lemon juice

2 teaspoons reduced-sodium soy sauce

1½ teaspoons grated fresh ginger

1 teaspoon Dijon mustard

1 teaspoon extra-virgin olive oil

1 bunch watercress, washed, tough stems removed

1 cup thinly sliced kirby or English cucumbers

Soak the sun-dried tomatoes in boiling water for a few minutes to soften them, then rinse and drain the tomatoes before cutting them up.

Hearty and light at the same time, warm salads are welcome in any weather. This one has a lovely balance of crisp and tender textures, spicy and fresh flavors, and a vibrant red-white-and-green color scheme: Slices of juicy garlic-rubbed steak are combined with penne, sun-dried tomatoes, watercress and cucumbers, and tossed with a soy-ginger-mustard dressing.

1 Bring a large covered pot of water to a boil over high heat. Preheat the broiler and a broiler pan and rack.

2 Put the dried tomatoes and water in a small saucepan and bring to a boil over high heat. Remove the pan from the heat, cover and let stand for 5 minutes, or until the tomatoes have softened. Drain the tomatoes in a small strainer, then rinse under cold running water until cool. Cut the tomatoes into small pieces.

3 Add the pasta to the boiling water, return to a boil and cook for 10 to 12 minutes or according to package directions until al dente. Drain in a colander and rinse briefly under cold running water; drain again.

4 Rub the steak with half of the garlic and all of the pepper. Place the steak on the broiler-pan rack and broil 4 to 6 inches from the heat for 5 minutes per side, or until medium-rare. Transfer the steak to a plate and let stand for 5 minutes while you make the dressing.

5 In a salad bowl, whisk together the broth, lemon juice, soy sauce, ginger, mustard, oil and the remaining garlic.

6 Transfer the steak to a cutting board. Add any juices that have collected on the plate to the salad dressing. Carve the steak into thin slices.

7 Add the pasta, dried tomatoes, watercress, cucumbers and steak to the salad bowl, and toss to mix.

Preparation time 15 minutes • **Total time** 35 minutes • **Per serving** 290 calories, 5.3 g. fat (17% of calories), 1.5 g. saturated fat, 38 mg. cholesterol, 223 mg. sodium, 3.9 g. dietary fiber, 80 mg. calcium, 4 mg. iron, 43 mg. vitamin C, 2 mg. beta-carotene
Serves 4

Pasta with Lamb and Rosemary Pesto

1 large lemon

6 ounces spinach, washed, tough stems removed

3 tablespoons defatted beef broth

½ teaspoon dried rosemary leaves

¼ teaspoon freshly ground black pepper

¼ teaspoon salt

⅛ teaspoon crushed red pepper flakes

1 garlic clove, peeled

8 ounces lean, trimmed, boneless lamb steak

8 ounces long fusilli or fettuccine

3 large carrots, halved lengthwise and cut into long diagonal slices

1 tablespoon grated Parmesan cheese

Use a small rubber spatula—or your hands—to spread the rosemary pesto over the lamb steak.

Pesto *alla Genovese*, known to every lover of Italian food, is made from basil, garlic, olive oil, Parmesan and pine nuts. Here is a very different pesto, composed of spinach, rosemary, garlic and lemon juice. The fragrant herb mixture is rubbed on lamb steak before it's broiled and is also tossed with the pasta.

1 Bring a large covered pot of water to a boil over high heat.

2 Meanwhile, with a swivel-bladed vegetable peeler, remove a 2-inch strip of zest from the lemon. Squeeze 2 tablespoons of juice from the lemon. Combine the lemon juice, spinach, broth, rosemary, black pepper, salt and crushed red pepper in a food processor. With the machine running, drop the lemon zest and the garlic through the feed tube and process until puréed.

3 Preheat the broiler, broiler pan and broiler rack. Place the lamb steak on a plate and spread 2 tablespoons of the rosemary pesto over it, coating both sides. Let stand for 5 minutes.

4 Place the lamb on the broiler-pan rack and broil 4 to 5 inches from the heat source for 4 to 5 minutes per side for medium-rare. Transfer to a clean plate and let stand for 5 minutes.

5 While the lamb broils, add the pasta to the boiling water, return to a boil and cook for 8 to 10 minutes or according to package directions until al dente. Three minutes before the pasta is done, add the carrots and cook until tender. Drain the pasta and carrots in a colander and transfer to a heated serving bowl. Toss the pasta and carrots with the remaining pesto.

6 Transfer the lamb to a cutting board. Pour any juices that have collected on the plate into the pasta. Carve the lamb into thin slices, place on top of the pasta and toss gently, then sprinkle with the Parmesan.

Preparation time 10 minutes • **Total time** 35 minutes • **Per serving** 351 calories, 6.1 g. fat (16% of calories), 2.1 g. saturated fat, 41 mg. cholesterol, 292 mg. sodium, 4.6 g. dietary fiber, 97 mg. calcium, 4 mg. iron, 20 mg. vitamin C, 14 mg. beta-carotene • **Serves 4**

❧ ❧ ❧

LEMONY ASPARAGUS AND PASTA SALAD

8 ounces penne pasta

1 pound asparagus, trimmed and cut diagonally into 2-inch pieces

2 tablespoons reduced-calorie mayonnaise

2 tablespoons defatted chicken broth or vegetable broth

1 tablespoon fresh lemon juice

2 teaspoons Dijon mustard

1 garlic clove, crushed

¼ teaspoon freshly ground black pepper

2 ounces shredded sharp Cheddar cheese

¼ cup diagonally sliced scallions

Cut the asparagus into pieces about the same size and shape as the penne.

Finding pasta shapes that echo other ingredients in a recipe is part of the fun of creative pasta cookery. Asparagus spears, cut into 2-inch lengths, are much the same shape as penne, or pasta "quills." Similarly, carrot slices would work well with rotelli, or wagon-wheel pasta, and ribbons of zucchini or yellow squash with fettuccine. Here, the asparagus and pasta are cooked together: Be sure to add the asparagus before the penne is done so that the pasta does not overcook.

1 Bring a large covered pot of water to a boil over high heat. Add the pasta, return to a boil and cook for 10 to 12 minutes or according to package directions until al dente. About three minutes before the pasta is done, add the asparagus and cook until crisp-tender. Drain the pasta and asparagus in a colander, cool under cold running water and drain again.

2 In a salad bowl, whisk together the mayonnaise, broth, lemon juice, mustard, garlic and pepper. Add the pasta and asparagus, and toss to coat well. Sprinkle with the Cheddar and scallions, and serve.

Preparation time 10 minutes • **Total time** 25 minutes • **Per serving** 309 calories, 7.9 g. fat (23% of calories), 3.6 g. saturated fat, 17 mg. cholesterol, 241 mg. sodium, 2.1 g. dietary fiber, 133 mg. calcium, 3 mg. iron, 23 mg. vitamin C, 0.4 mg. beta-carotene • **Serves 4**

❧ ❧ ❧

SUBSTITUTION
Frozen asparagus can be used when fresh is not available. It's not necessary to cook the asparagus along with the pasta; just thaw it in the refrigerator, then place it in a colander and pour the boiling cooking liquid over it when you drain the pasta.

MARKET AND PANTRY
Asparagus can be expensive, so you want to be sure to get the best spears with the least waste. Look for plump stalks that

are fresh and green all the way down: If the bottom of the stalk is hard, dry and white, it will be unusable. The tips of the spears should consist of tightly closed, moist-looking buds. The best way to store this delicate vegetable is to treat it as if it were a bouquet of flowers: Trim the bottoms of the stalks, then stand them in a tall container and add 1 inch of cold water. Cover with a plastic bag to hold in the moisture. Fresh asparagus will keep for about 3 days in the refrigerator.

Pasta with Cauliflower and Cheddar

8 ounces whole-wheat linguine

3 cups small cauliflower florets

1½ cups 1% low-fat milk

2 tablespoons cornstarch

½ teaspoon dry mustard

½ teaspoon freshly ground black pepper

¼ teaspoon dried thyme, crumbled

¼ teaspoon hot pepper sauce

⅛ teaspoon salt

4 ounces extra-sharp Cheddar cheese, shredded

2 tablespoons grated Parmesan cheese

¼ cup thinly sliced scallion greens

Ivory white cauliflower could almost pass for pasta, especially when blanketed with a creamy sauce, and it makes a most interesting meal when paired with sturdy whole-wheat linguine. Some "secret ingredients" help cut the fat content of the two-cheese sauce: It's based on a blend of low-fat milk and cornstarch (rather than whole milk), and the sharp Cheddar flavor is underscored with dry mustard and hot pepper sauce so that you use less cheese than usual.

1 Bring a large covered pot of water to a boil over high heat. Add the pasta, return to a boil and cook for 9 to 11 minutes, or according to package directions. Four minutes before the pasta is done, stir in the cauliflower and cook until the cauliflower is tender and the pasta is al dente. Reserving ½ cup of the cooking liquid, drain the pasta and cauliflower in a colander.

2 While the pasta is cooking, in a heavy medium saucepan, whisk together the milk, cornstarch, mustard, pepper, thyme, hot pepper sauce and salt until smooth. Place the pan over medium-high heat and bring to a boil, stirring constantly. Cook, stirring, for 1 minute, or until the sauce is quite thick; remove the pan from the heat.

3 Transfer the pasta and cauliflower to a warmed serving bowl; add the reserved pasta cooking liquid and toss to mix well.

4 Add the Cheddar and Parmesan to the sauce and whisk until smooth. Pour the sauce over the pasta and cauliflower, and toss to mix. Sprinkle with the scallions.

Preparation time 10 minutes • **Total time** 30 minutes • **Per serving** 401 calories, 12 g. fat (27% of calories), 7.3 g. saturated fat, 36 mg. cholesterol, 373 mg. sodium, 8.7 g. dietary fiber, 412 mg. calcium, 3 mg. iron, 56 mg. vitamin C, 0.3 mg. beta-carotene • **Serves 4**

KITCHEN TIPS
You'll need a head of cauliflower that weighs about 2 pounds to yield the 3 cups of florets required for this recipe. Take off any leaves and wash the head of cauliflower. Halve it, using a large, heavy knife, then remove the dense core. Break the head into large florets or cut them apart with a small knife. Then, if necessary, divide the florets into smaller sections.

PENNE WITH BROCCOLI AND CHICK-PEAS

1 tablespoon extra-virgin olive oil

2 large red onions, sliced

3 garlic cloves, minced

4 cups small broccoli florets

1 cup defatted reduced-sodium chicken broth or vegetable broth

8 ounces penne pasta

1 can (10½ ounces) chick-peas, rinsed and drained or 1¼ cups drained cooked chick-peas (see below)

½ teaspoon freshly ground black pepper

3 tablespoons freshly grated Parmesan cheese

If using dried chick-peas (see directions at right), drain the soaking water and then add fresh water for cooking. This helps make the chick-peas easier to digest.

Chick-peas are a favorite legume around the Mediterranean. They are the main ingredient in the Middle Eastern fritters called *falafel* as well as *hummus*, a rich, creamy paste used as a sandwich spread or dip. The French prepare many soups, stews and salads with these nutty-tasting legumes, and a savory oversized pancake called *socca*, beloved in Nice, is made from chick-pea flour.

1 Bring a large covered pot of water to a boil over high heat.

2 Meanwhile, heat the oil in a large, deep skillet over high heat. Add the onions and garlic, and stir well to coat with the oil. Reduce the heat to medium and cook, stirring frequently, for 7 to 8 minutes, or until the onions are very tender and light golden brown. (Add a tablespoon of the broth if the pan gets too dry.)

3 Stir in the broccoli and broth; increase the heat to high and bring to a boil. Reduce the heat to medium-high, cover and simmer, stirring occasionally, for 6 to 7 minutes, or until the broccoli is tender.

4 Meanwhile, add the pasta to the boiling water, return to a boil and cook for 10 to 12 minutes or according to package directions until al dente. Reserving ¼ cup of the cooking liquid, drain the pasta in a colander.

5 Add the chick-peas and pepper to the broccoli and cook for 2 to 3 minutes, or until heated through. Add the penne and the reserved cooking liquid to the vegetables, and toss to coat the pasta. Transfer the mixture to a heated serving bowl and sprinkle with the Parmesan.

Preparation time 10 minutes • **Total time** 35 minutes • **Per serving** 404 calories, 7.7 g. fat (17% of calories), 1.6 g. saturated fat, 4 mg. cholesterol, 366 mg. sodium, 9.7 g. dietary fiber, 172 mg. calcium, 4 mg. iron, 102 mg. vitamin C, 1.3 mg. beta-carotene • **Serves 4**

KITCHEN TIP

Here's how to presoak and cook dried chick-peas: Place them in a large saucepan and add cold water to cover. Bring to a boil and cook for 2 minutes; cover and let stand for 1 hour. Drain, add fresh water (2 cups for each ½ cup of chick-peas) and bring to a boil. Simmer, partially covered, for about 90 minutes, or until the chick-peas are tender but firm.

MACARONI AND CHEESE SALAD

6 ounces elbow macaroni

⅓ cup chopped fresh cilantro

¼ cup hot or medium salsa

3 tablespoons reduced-fat sour cream

Grated zest of 1 lime

2 tablespoons fresh lime juice

1 teaspoon ground cumin

½ teaspoon freshly ground black pepper

1 medium green bell pepper, diced

1 medium yellow or red bell pepper, diced

2 ounces shredded sharp Cheddar cheese

½ cup sliced scallions

Instead of a mayonnaise-dressed pasta salad, enliven your next buffet or barbecue with this colorful macaroni-and-vegetable mixture. Like the best party dishes, it can be made a day in advance, and the flavor will intensify if you prepare the salad ahead of time and refrigerate it overnight.

1 Bring a large covered pot of water to a boil over high heat. Add the pasta to the boiling water, return to a boil and cook for 7 to 9 minutes or according to package directions until al dente. Drain in a colander and rinse under cold running water; drain again.

2 While the pasta is cooking, in a salad bowl, whisk together the cilantro, salsa, sour cream, lime zest and juice, cumin and black pepper.

3 Add the macaroni, bell peppers, Cheddar and scallions to the dressing, and toss to combine.

Preparation time 12 minutes • **Total time** 25 minutes • **Per serving** 257 calories, 7 g. fat (25% of calories), 3.8 g. saturated fat, 19 mg. cholesterol, 185 mg. sodium, 2 g. dietary fiber, 131 mg. calcium, 3 mg. iron, 68 mg. vitamin C, 0.9 mg. beta-carotene **Serves 4**

This citrus zester shaves fine shreds of zest that are easy to measure in a spoon. Press the tool firmly against the fruit and pull it toward you.

This utensil, called a channel knife, cuts a thicker strip of zest, which can be chopped into smaller pieces for recipes or left whole for garnishing.

GREEK-STYLE PASTA AND TOMATO SALAD

8 ounces corkscrew pasta

2½ ounces crumbled feta cheese

⅓ cup plain nonfat yogurt

1 tablespoon fresh lemon juice

¾ teaspoon dried mint

¼ teaspoon ground cumin

¼ teaspoon freshly ground black pepper

⅛ teaspoon salt

1 garlic clove, peeled

1 bunch watercress, washed, tough stems removed

2 cups halved cherry tomatoes

½ cup sliced radishes

Most people have sampled Greek salad, a flavorful toss of greens, cucumbers, tomatoes, ripe olives and tangy feta cheese with a dressing made of Greek olive oil, lemon juice and oregano. For this hearty pasta salad, feta cheese is used in a creamy yogurt-based dressing that is served over pasta, watercress, tomatoes and radishes.

1 Bring a large covered pot of water to a boil over high heat. Add the pasta to the boiling water, return to a boil and cook for 11 to 13 minutes or according to package directions until al dente. Drain in a colander and rinse under cold running water; drain again. Transfer to a salad bowl.

2 While the pasta cooks, combine the feta, yogurt, lemon juice, mint, cumin, pepper and salt in a food processor or blender. With the machine running, drop the garlic clove through the feed tube and process until the dressing is smooth.

3 Pour the dressing over the pasta. Add the watercress, cherry tomatoes and radishes, and toss to coat well.

Preparation time 15 minutes • **Total time** 30 minutes • **Per serving** 288 calories, 5 g. fat (16% of calories), 2.8 g. saturated fat, 16 mg. cholesterol, 311 mg. sodium, 3.3 g. dietary fiber, 195 mg. calcium, 3 mg. iron, 33 mg. vitamin C, 1.4 mg. beta-carotene
Serves 4

Cut the thick stems from the watercress at the point where the bunch is tied.

Holding the cress by the remaining stems, rinse the leaves in a basin of water.

RAVIOLI WITH PEAS AND RED PEPPERS

½ cup defatted reduced-sodium chicken broth

1 package (10 ounces) frozen peas

¼ cup loosely packed Italian parsley sprigs

1 garlic clove, peeled

¼ teaspoon freshly ground black pepper

9 ounces fresh or frozen cheese ravioli

1 medium red bell pepper, diced

2 teaspoons grated Parmesan cheese

You don't need to make your own pasta in order to serve it fresh: Small pasta shops are springing up everywhere, offering such specialties as pumpkin ravioli, wild-mushroom tortellini and broccoli-rabe agnolotti. Cooking times vary for filled pastas; you need to know the approximate time in advance so you can cook the bell peppers and peas in the same pot as the ravioli without overcooking either the vegetables or the pasta. If directions don't come with fresh ravioli, be sure to ask about the recommended cooking time.

1 Bring a large covered pot of water to a boil over high heat.

2 Meanwhile, in a small saucepan, combine the broth, 1 cup of the peas, the parsley sprigs and garlic. Cover and bring to a boil over high heat. Cook for 1 minute; remove from the heat.

3 Purée the pea mixture in a food processor or blender until very smooth; stir in the black pepper and set aside.

4 Add the ravioli to the boiling water and return to a boil, stirring frequently. Cook for 4 to 5 minutes, or according to package directions. Two minutes before the ravioli are done, add the bell peppers and the remaining 1 cup peas to the pot. Return to a boil and cook for 2 minutes longer, or until the peppers are crisp-tender, the peas are heated through, and the ravioli are tender. Drain in a colander and transfer to a warmed serving bowl.

5 Add the pea purée to the ravioli and toss gently to combine. Sprinkle with the Parmesan.

Preparation time 12 minutes • **Total time** 30 minutes • **Per serving** 272 calories, 9 g. fat (30% of calories), 4.7 g. saturated fat, 57 mg. cholesterol, 450 mg. sodium, 3.2 g. dietary fiber, 188 mg. calcium, 3 mg. iron, 52 mg. vitamin C, 1.1 mg. beta-carotene
Serves 4

KITCHEN TIPS
It's not necessary to thaw frozen peas, and they will probably turn mushy if you do. The peas take only minutes to cook, and if you're using them in a salad, you don't even need to cook them—just place them in a strainer and rinse them under cold tap water. Frozen peas straight from the freezer are a great snack—one even vegetable-spurning kids may like.

Pasta Salad with Chick-Peas

1 pound ripe tomatoes

1 medium cucumber, peeled and diced

¼ cup chopped red onions

2 tablespoons chopped fresh dill

2 tablespoons chopped fresh mint

1 tablespoon extra-virgin olive oil

1 tablespoon red wine vinegar

1 small garlic clove, crushed

½ teaspoon freshly ground black pepper

¼ teaspoon salt

1 can (19 ounces) chick-peas, rinsed and drained

8 ounces fresh spinach linguine, cut in half

You'll find fresh pasta in many supermarkets, in the dairy section or in a special display with ready-made sauces. If you don't use fresh pasta right away, wrap it airtight and store it in the refrigerator for up to one week or in the freezer for up to a month.

1 Bring a medium saucepan of water to a boil over high heat. One at a time, add the tomatoes and blanch for 20 seconds, or until the skins begin to wrinkle. Cool the tomatoes in a bowl of cold water and slip off the skins. Coarsely chop the tomatoes and place in a salad bowl.

2 Add the cucumber, onions, dill, mint, oil, vinegar, garlic, pepper and salt to the tomatoes, and mix well; stir in the chick-peas. Cover and let stand at room temperature for 10 minutes.

3 Return the water in the pot to a boil, add the pasta and bring to a boil again. Cook, stirring frequently, for 3 to 5 minutes, or until the pasta floats to the surface and is al dente. Drain in a colander and rinse briefly under cold running water.

4 Add the pasta to the chick-pea mixture and toss thoroughly.

Preparation time 15 minutes • **Total time** 35 minutes • **Per serving** 323 calories, 8.2 g. fat (23% of calories), 0.7 g. saturated fat, 64 mg. cholesterol, 345 mg. sodium, 5.4 g. dietary fiber, 87 mg. calcium, 4 mg. iron, 28 mg. vitamin C, 0.5 mg. beta-carotene • **Serves 4**

❧ ❧ ❧

Drop a tomato into the pot of boiling water; remove it when the skin wrinkles.

After the tomato has cooled slightly, you can easily peel off the skin.

TURKEY TETRAZZINI

8 ounces wide egg noodles

1½ cups defatted reduced-sodium chicken broth

1 cup 1% low-fat milk

3 tablespoons cornstarch

½ teaspoon freshly ground black pepper

½ teaspoon dried thyme, crumbled

⅛ teaspoon salt

4 tablespoons grated Parmesan cheese

1½ teaspoons dry sherry (optional)

1 tablespoon unsalted butter or margarine

8 ounces fresh mushrooms, sliced

¾ cup thinly sliced scallions

4 ounces skinless roast turkey breast, cut into matchstick strips about the same length as the noodles

The name of Italian opera diva Luisa Tetrazzini lives on in the baked pasta dish created in her honor. An admiring chef devised a dinner of spaghetti, chicken and mushrooms in a sherried cream sauce, topped with Parmesan and baked until golden. Turkey is often substituted for chicken in the dish; to lighten this particular rendition, a mixture of low-fat milk and cornstarch takes the place of the cream sauce.

1 Preheat the oven to 450°. Spray a 9 x 9-inch or 11 x 7-inch baking dish with no-stick spray.

2 Bring a large covered pot of water to a boil over high heat. Add the noodles to the boiling water, return to a boil and cook for 5 to 6 minutes (the noodles should be slightly underdone). Drain in a colander and rinse briefly under gently running cold water to keep the noodles from sticking; drain again.

3 Meanwhile, in a medium saucepan, whisk together the broth, milk, cornstarch, pepper, thyme and salt. Bring to a boil over high heat, whisking constantly. Cook, stirring, until the sauce is thickened and smooth. Remove from the heat and stir in 3 tablespoons of the Parmesan and the sherry (if using).

4 In the pasta cooking pot, melt the butter or margarine over medium-high heat. Add the mushrooms and scallions, and sauté for 2 to 4 minutes, or until the mushrooms are tender (the pan will be dry at first; keep stirring and the mushrooms will release their liquid). Remove the pot from the heat and stir in the noodles, sauce and turkey. Toss until mixed, then transfer to the prepared pan.

5 Sprinkle the surface with the remaining 1 tablespoon Parmesan. Bake for 15 minutes, or until the sauce is bubbly and the top of the casserole is lightly browned.

Preparation time 10 minutes • **Total time** 45 minutes • **Per serving** 397 calories, 10 g. fat (23% of calories), 4.3 g. saturated fat, 91 mg. cholesterol, 493 mg. sodium, 2.8 g. dietary fiber, 206 mg. calcium, 4 mg. iron, 6 mg. vitamin C, 0.2 mg. beta-carotene • **Serves 4**

❧ ❧ ❧

Pasta with Escarole and Cannellini

1 tablespoon extra-virgin olive oil

1 medium onion, chopped

1 large carrot, diced

2 large celery stalks with leaves, diced

3–4 garlic cloves, crushed

½–¾ teaspoon freshly ground black pepper

½ teaspoon dried basil, crumbled

¼ teaspoon salt

6 cups loosely packed cut escarole (1-inch pieces), well washed

½ cup defatted chicken or vegetable broth

1 can (19 ounces) cannellini beans, rinsed and drained

8 ounces pasta twists

Escarole's ruffled pale-green leaves have a slight bitterness reminiscent of the taste of chicory, a close relative. The inner leaves have a milder flavor than the outer leaves. Although escarole is often used in salads, it is delicious when braised in broth and served as a side dish or, as it is here, partnered with pasta and white beans.

1 Bring a large covered pot of water to a boil over high heat.

2 Meanwhile, warm the oil in a large, heavy saucepan over medium-high heat. Stir in the onions, carrots, celery and garlic, and sauté for 1 minute. Add the pepper, basil and salt, and reduce the heat to medium-low; cover and cook, stirring frequently, for 5 to 7 minutes, or until the vegetables are tender.

3 Add the escarole and broth to the vegetables, and raise the heat to high. Cook, tossing frequently, for 2 to 3 minutes, or until the escarole is wilted. Stir in the beans and reduce the heat to medium; cover and simmer for 3 to 5 minutes, or until the beans are heated through.

4 Meanwhile, add the pasta to the boiling water, return to a boil and cook for 10 to 12 minutes or according to package directions until al dente. Reserving 2 tablespoons of the cooking liquid, drain the pasta in a colander.

5 Combine the pasta, the reserved cooking liquid and the escarole mixture in a heated serving bowl, and toss to combine well.

Preparation time 15 minutes • **Total time** 35 minutes • **Per serving** 390 calories, 5.6 g. fat (13% of calories), 0.7 g. saturated fat, 0 mg. cholesterol, 483 mg. sodium, 11 g. dietary fiber, 126 mg. calcium, 5 mg. iron, 15 mg. vitamin C, 5.4 mg. beta-carotene • **Serves 4**

FOR A CHANGE
Fennel, which is very similar to celery in texture, has a mild licorice-like flavor that would add a new dimension to this dish. Use 1 cup of diced fennel to replace the celery.

NUTRITION NOTE
When choosing greens, the general rule is: The darker the leaves, the more nutritious. Escarole, for instance, is a richer source of beta-carotene, vitamin C and calcium than iceberg lettuce.

PICNIC MACARONI-TUNA SALAD

6 ounces elbow macaroni

¼ cup plain nonfat yogurt

2 tablespoons reduced-calorie mayonnaise

2 tablespoons snipped fresh dill

2 tablespoons red wine vinegar

1 teaspoon Dijon mustard

½ teaspoon freshly ground black pepper

1 can (6⅛ ounces) water-packed tuna, drained

1 can (15 ounces) black beans, rinsed and drained

1 medium red bell pepper, diced

2 large celery stalks, sliced

¼ cup sliced radishes

¼ cup chopped red onion

Just about any mayonnaise-based salad dressing can be lightened by substituting low-fat or nonfat yogurt for all or some of the mayo. In this case, nonfat yogurt is combined with reduced-calorie mayonnaise; the addition of fresh dill, vinegar and mustard ensures that not a bit of flavor is lost even though the fat content is considerably reduced. Crunchy celery, bell peppers, radishes and red onion add up to an unusually appetizing macaroni salad, and black beans make this dish a nutritional superstar.

1 Bring a large covered pot of water to a boil over high heat. Add the pasta, return to a boil and cook for 8 to 9 minutes or according to package directions until al dente. Drain in a colander and cool briefly under gently running cold water; drain again.

2 In a salad bowl, whisk together the yogurt, mayonnaise, dill, vinegar, mustard and black pepper.

3 Break the tuna into flakes and put it in a small strainer. Rinse under cold running water and drain well.

4 Add the macaroni, tuna, beans, bell peppers, celery, radishes and onions to the salad bowl, and toss to coat with the dressing.

Preparation time 23 minutes • **Total time** 35 minutes • **Per serving** 314 calories, 3.6 g. fat (10% of calories), 0.7 g. saturated fat, 19 mg. cholesterol, 427 mg. sodium, 5 g. dietary fiber, 86 mg. calcium, 5 mg. iron, 41 mg. vitamin C, 0.7 mg. beta-carotene
Serves 4

Kitchen shears or regular scissors make quick work of mincing herbs such as dill. Pat the herbs thoroughly dry after rinsing them so that the leaves do not stick to the scissor blades.

ON THE MENU
Serve the salad on a bed of curly greens and accompany it with wedges of juicy ripe tomato.

NUTRITION NOTE
The majority of Americans don't need to worry about consuming too much protein; in fact, most get more protein than necessary, with an unfortunate bonus of saturated fat and cholesterol if red meat is the main source of protein. This macaroni salad is a fine example of a more healthful way to eat protein: One serving supplies 22 grams of protein, or about half the daily requirement for the average woman, but has less than 4 grams of fat. Most of the protein in the salad comes from the tuna, macaroni and beans. These ingredients also provide good amounts of iron, a mineral that many people think they can get only by eating red meat.

MEDITERRANEAN SEASHELL SALAD

- 2 **tablespoons frozen apple juice concentrate**
- 2 **tablespoons chopped fresh Italian parsley**
- 1 **tablespoon coarse Dijon mustard**
- 1 **tablespoon extra-virgin olive oil**
- 1 **tablespoon red wine vinegar**
- ½ **teaspoon ground cumin**
- ¼ **teaspoon freshly ground black pepper**
- 1 **medium yellow or red bell pepper, thinly sliced**
- 1 **cup thinly sliced fennel or celery**
- ¼ **cup thinly sliced red onions**
- 6 **ounces medium pasta shells**
- 3 **tablespoons golden raisins**
- 1 **can (3¾ ounces) water-pack sardines, drained and gently rinsed**

Fresh sardines, quickly grilled, broiled or fried, are a great delicacy, and the tiny iridescent fish are a highlight of summer meals around the Mediterranean basin. In Sicily, filleted sardines are combined with macaroni, sweet fennel, onions, pine nuts and golden raisins—a typically Sicilian juxtaposition of sweet and savory flavors—in a casserole called *pasta con le sarde.* This unbaked version of the dish is made with canned sardines and a sprightly apple-juice dressing. A timesaving trick: The raisins are plumped by adding them to the pasta during the last few moments of cooking time.

1 Bring a large covered pot of water to a boil over high heat.

2 Meanwhile, in a salad bowl, whisk together the apple juice concentrate, parsley, mustard, oil, vinegar, cumin and black pepper.

3 Add the bell peppers, fennel or celery and onions to the dressing, and stir to blend. Cover and let stand at room temperature for 10 minutes.

4 While the vegetables marinate, add the pasta to the boiling water, return to a boil and cook for 9 to 11 minutes or according to package directions until al dente. One minute before the pasta is done, add the raisins. Drain the pasta and raisins in a colander, rinse briefly under cold running water and drain again.

5 Add the pasta and raisins to the salad bowl, and toss to mix. Add the sardines and toss gently.

Preparation time 10 minutes • **Total time** 25 minutes • **Per serving** 303 calories, 9.1 g. fat (27% of calories), 0.6 g. saturated fat, 0 mg. cholesterol, 178 mg. sodium, 2.2 g. dietary fiber, 111 mg. calcium, 3 mg. iron, 49 mg. vitamin C, 0.7 mg. beta-carotene • **Serves 4**

❧ ❧ ❧

A fennel bulb, like a bunch of celery, is made up of many layers, so when you slice it crosswise it will fall into thin strips.

NUTRITION NOTE
Sardines have a lot to offer nutritionally. Although they are higher in fat than tuna, the fat is rich in omega-3s, polyunsaturated fatty acids that may be protective against heart disease. In addition, sardines are rich in iron, and the bone-in types are an excellent source of calcium.

LINGUINE WITH SMOKED SALMON

8 **ounces spinach linguine or regular linguine**

¼ **cup reduced-fat sour cream**

3 **tablespoons snipped fresh dill**

2 **teaspoons distilled white vinegar**

1½ **teaspoons bottled white horseradish**

¼ **teaspoon freshly ground black pepper**

⅛ **teaspoon salt**

1½ **cups halved yellow or red pear tomatoes, plum tomatoes or cherry tomatoes**

1 **cup thinly sliced kirby or hothouse cucumber**

3 **ounces sliced smoked salmon, cut into thin strips**

⅓ **cup thinly sliced scallions**

Gourmet shops and even supermarket deli counters and mail-order gourmet catalogues offer a number of choices in smoked salmon. You can go the economy route and buy what's called lox—salty brine-cured salmon—or be a bit more extravagant, since the recipe calls for only three ounces of fish. Some of the pricier choices are cold-smoked "Nova," a domestic product; imported Scottish smoked salmon (or "Scottish-style" salmon prepared on this side of the Atlantic) and alder-smoked salmon from the Pacific Northwest.

1 Bring a large covered pot of water to a boil over high heat. Add the pasta, return to a boil and cook for 9 to 11 minutes or according to package directions until al dente. Drain in a colander, cool briefly under cold running water and drain again.

2 In a salad bowl, combine the sour cream, dill, vinegar, horseradish, pepper and salt, and whisk with a fork until blended. Add the drained pasta, the tomatoes, cucumbers, salmon and scallions, and toss gently but thoroughly.

Preparation time 15 minutes • **Total time** 25 minutes • **Per serving** 284 calories, 4.1 g. fat (13% of calories), 1.4 g. saturated fat, 10 mg. cholesterol, 267 mg. sodium, 7.4 g. dietary fiber, 61 mg. calcium, 2 mg. iron, 16 mg. vitamin C, 0.3 mg. beta-carotene • **Serves 4**

FOR A CHANGE
Smoked trout could stand in for the smoked salmon, but be particularly gentle when tossing the pasta, as the trout will break apart more readily than salmon.

ON THE MENU
A crisp *ficelle*—a long, thin loaf of French bread—would be welcome with this pasta. For dessert, fill a glass bowl with well-chilled melon balls tossed with fresh mint.

Joining the ever-popular cherry tomatoes as appealing garnishes and ingredients are diminutive yellow pear tomatoes, which you may find in farmers' markets in midsummer.

Pasta Caesar Salad with Chicken

3 tablespoons nonfat mayonnaise

1 ounce Parmesan cheese, coarsely grated

2 tablespoons Italian parsley sprigs

1 tablespoon plus 1 teaspoon fresh lemon juice

1 tablespoon defatted reduced-sodium chicken broth

2 garlic cloves, crushed

1 teaspoon anchovy paste

½ teaspoon freshly ground black pepper

6 ounces cavatappi pasta

8 ounces thin-sliced chicken cutlets, cut into 1-inch pieces

⅛ teaspoon salt

1 bunch arugula or watercress, washed, tough stems removed

Caesar salad is said to have been created in the 1920s by chef Caesar Cardini, owner of a restaurant in Tijuana, Mexico. The greens, garlicky dressing and a lightly cooked egg are often tossed together with a flourish at tableside. For this variation, Caesar dressing, flavored with anchovy paste and Parmesan, is tossed with pasta, tart greens and morsels of broiled chicken.

1 Bring a large covered pot of water to a boil over high heat. Preheat the broiler. Spray a jelly-roll pan with no-stick spray.

2 Meanwhile, combine the mayonnaise, 1 tablespoon of the Parmesan, the parsley sprigs, 1 tablespoon of the lemon juice, the broth, half of the garlic, the anchovy paste and ¼ teaspoon of the pepper in a food processor or blender, and process until smooth.

3 Add the pasta to the boiling water, return to a boil and cook for 8 to 10 minutes or according to package directions until al dente. Drain in a colander and cool briefly under cold running water; drain again.

4 Place the chicken in the prepared pan. Drizzle the remaining 1 teaspoon lemon juice over the chicken. Sprinkle with the remaining crushed garlic, the remaining ¼ teaspoon pepper and the salt, and toss to mix. Broil 3 to 4 inches from the heat for 3 to 5 minutes, or until the chicken is cooked through and lightly browned. Remove from the heat.

5 Transfer the pasta to a salad bowl. Add the arugula or watercress, the dressing, the chicken and any juices that have collected in the pan, and the remaining Parmesan. Toss to coat well.

Preparation time 15 minutes • **Total time** 30 minutes • **Per serving** 274 calories, 3.9 g. fat (13% of calories), 1.7 g. saturated fat, 39 mg. cholesterol, 394 mg. sodium, 2.1 g. dietary fiber, 172 mg. calcium, 2 mg. iron, 23 mg. vitamin C, 1.3 mg. beta-carotene • **Serves 4**

GARLICKY SPAGHETTI WITH TURKEY

8 ounces perciatelli or spaghetti

8 ounces green beans, trimmed and cut in half

1 tablespoon plus 1 teaspoon extra-virgin olive oil

½ teaspoon crushed red pepper flakes

3 garlic cloves, crushed

6 ounces julienne-cut skinless roast turkey breast

¾ cup julienne-cut roasted red peppers (freshly roasted or from a jar)

1 tablespoon cider vinegar

¼ teaspoon salt

Store-bought roasted peppers are a convenience, but nothing rivals the flavor of freshly roasted bell peppers. The method shown below is simple and quick, using quartered, stemmed and seeded peppers rather than whole ones.

1 Bring a large covered pot of water to a boil over high heat.

2 Add the pasta to the boiling water, return to a boil and cook for 10 to 12 minutes or according to package directions until al dente. About 5 minutes before the pasta is cooked, add the beans and cook until the pasta is al dente and the beans are crisp-tender. Drain in a colander and transfer to a large serving bowl.

3 In a small skillet, stir together the oil and pepper flakes. Place over medium heat and cook, stirring constantly, for 2 minutes. Stir in the garlic and cook, stirring constantly, for 30 seconds, or until fragrant. Immediately pour the hot oil mixture over the pasta and beans.

4 Add the turkey, red peppers, vinegar and salt to the pasta mixture, and toss to combine.

Preparation time 10 minutes • **Total time** 30 minutes • **Per serving** 350 calories, 7.7 g. fat (20% of calories), 1.5 g. saturated fat, 33 mg. cholesterol, 179 mg. sodium, 2.3 g. dietary fiber, 47 mg. calcium, 4 mg. iron, 40 mg. vitamin C, 0.8 mg. beta-carotene • **Serves 4**

❧ ❧ ❧

Arrange quartered, stemmed, seeded peppers, skin-side up, on a foil-lined baking pan. Broil until well charred.

Place the roasted peppers in a bowl and cover it. Let the peppers steam for a few minutes to loosen their skins.

Scrape off the charred skin with a table knife. If neccessary, rub off stubborn patches of char under cold running water.

SMOKED TURKEY CARBONARA

8 ounces linguine

8 ounces asparagus, sliced diagonally into 1-inch pieces

2 large eggs

3 large egg whites

¼ cup skim milk

2 tablespoons grated Parmesan cheese

2 tablespoons chopped fresh Italian parsley

½ teaspoon freshly ground black pepper

⅛ teaspoon salt

Large pinch of ground nutmeg, preferably freshly grated

Large pinch of ground red pepper

3 ounces smoked turkey, cut into julienne

1 tablespoon olive oil

The term *carbonara* describes dishes cooked with bacon or ham; the best-known of these dishes is *pasta alla carbonara*, a luxuriously rich creation that calls for pancetta (an Italian cured bacon), Parmesan or Romano cheese, heavy cream—and one whole egg per serving. For this version, smoked turkey stands in for pancetta and skim milk substitutes for cream; two eggs (combined with two egg whites, which are virtually fat-free) serve four.

1 Bring a large covered pot of water to a boil over high heat. Add the pasta to the boiling water, return to a boil and cook, stirring frequently, for 9 to 11 minutes or according to package directions. Two minutes before the pasta is done, add the asparagus and cook until the asparagus is crisp-tender and the pasta is al dente. Drain the pasta and asparagus in a colander and rinse briefly under cold running water; drain again.

2 In a large bowl, whisk together the eggs, egg whites, milk, Parmesan, parsley, black pepper, salt, nutmeg and red pepper until well blended. Stir in the turkey. Add the pasta and asparagus, and toss, using 2 spoons, until the spaghetti is coated with the egg mixture.

3 In a large no-stick skillet, warm the oil over high heat. Add the pasta mixture and cook, tossing constantly with 2 wooden spoons, for 2 to 3 minutes, or until the eggs have set into small clumps and the pasta is hot.

Preparation time 10 minutes • **Total time** 20 minutes • **Per serving** 347 calories, 8.5 g. fat (22% of calories), 2.2 g. saturated fat, 120 mg. cholesterol, 428 mg. sodium, 2.1 g. dietary fiber, 103 mg. calcium, 3 mg. iron, 21 mg. vitamin C, 0.5 mg. beta-carotene • **Serves 4**

❧ ❧ ❧

Intensely fragrant freshly grated nutmeg makes a tremendous difference in both savory and sweet dishes. This miniature grater is specially made for nutmeg.

KITCHEN TIPS

Cooking the asparagus in the same pot with the pasta is a time-saver, but be sure to add the asparagus gradually so the water does not stop boiling.

MARKET AND PANTRY

Smoked turkey, cured over flavorful woods such as mesquite or apple, is widely available. Keep it well wrapped so its assertive aroma does not permeate other foods.

PART 5
Side Dishes & Vegetables

SPICY GREEN BEANS WITH ANCHOVIES

1 cup water

½ cup sun-dried tomatoes (not oil-packed)

1 garlic clove, peeled

1 pound green beans, trimmed and halved crosswise

2 tablespoons chopped Italian parsley

4 anchovy fillets, rinsed, patted dry and chopped

1 tablespoon balsamic vinegar

1 teaspoon extra-virgin olive oil

⅛ teaspoon salt

⅛ teaspoon freshly ground black pepper

⅛ teaspoon crushed red pepper flakes, or more to taste

This unusual vegetable combination could fit into several different places in a traditional Italian menu: Offer it as an appetizer, as a side dish, or, atop a bed of greens, as a salad course, served after the main dish. And the beans are equally good hot or cold. If anchovies are not to your liking, simply leave them out.

1 In a small saucepan, bring the water to a boil over high heat. Remove the pan from the heat, stir in the sun-dried tomatoes, cover and let stand for 8 to 10 minutes, or until the tomatoes are softened. Reserving 2 tablespoons of the soaking liquid, drain the tomatoes, and cut into small pieces with kitchen shears, or chop with a knife.

2 Pour ½ inch of water into a large, deep skillet; cover and bring to a boil over high heat. Add the garlic and cook for 1 minute; remove with a slotted spoon and set aside. Add the green beans to the skillet, return to a boil and cook, uncovered, for 5 to 6 minutes, or until the beans are tender. Drain the beans in a colander.

3 While the beans are cooking, in a serving bowl, combine the parsley, anchovies, vinegar, oil, salt, black pepper, red pepper flakes and the reserved 2 tablespoons soaking liquid. Using a garlic press, crush the garlic clove into the bowl and stir well to combine.

4 Add the beans and sun-dried tomatoes to the bowl, and toss to coat.

Preparation time 10 minutes • **Total time** 20 minutes • **Per serving** 73 calories, 1.6 g. fat (20% of calories), 0.3 g. saturated fat, 2 mg. cholesterol, 230 mg. sodium, 3.3 g. dietary fiber, 51 mg. calcium, 1 mg. iron, 18 mg. vitamin C, 0.5 mg. beta-carotene • **Serves 4**

FOOD FACT
Although you can now buy balsamic vinegar in supermarkets, its price will never be comparable with that of more common vinegars. (The finest balsamic vinegars inhabit the same price range as superb vintage wines.) Why spend dollars on a bottle of balsamic when you can get a pint of cider vinegar for pennies? Because no other vinegar has its sweet, complex flavor, and none is so carefully made. Only sweet trebbiano grapes go into balsamic vinegar, which is aged for at least 12 years in wooden casks. To get an authentic balsamic, bottled in Italy, look for a code on the label: Vinegars labeled API MO are from Modena, while those marked API RE are from Reggio.

Parmesan-Baked Plum Tomatoes

8 medium plum tomatoes (about 1¼ pounds)

¼ teaspoon salt

⅛ teaspoon freshly ground black pepper

¾ teaspoon olive oil

16 small fresh basil leaves

2 tablespoons unseasoned dry breadcrumbs

1 tablespoon grated Parmesan cheese

As with so many other everyday kitchen tasks, your finger is the best tool for spreading the oil over the tomatoes.

Baked tomato halves are eaten all over Italy; plum tomatoes, which are less watery than spherical tomatoes, are especially good when cooked by this method. Some traditional recipes call for the tomatoes to bake in a deep pool of olive oil, but here the tops are rubbed with just a little oil. The baking time will depend to some extent on the ripeness of the tomatoes: If they are very ripe, check them for doneness a little sooner in the second phase of baking.

1 Preheat the the oven to 425°. Spray a jelly-roll pan with no-stick spray.

2 Cut the tomatoes in half lengthwise, trimming the stem ends, if desired. Arrange the tomatoes, cut-side-up, in a single layer in the prepared pan. Sprinkle the tomatoes with the salt and black pepper, then drizzle with the oil. With your finger, spread the oil and seasonings evenly over the surface of the tomatoes. Place a basil leaf on top of each tomato half.

3 In a cup, mix the breadcrumbs and Parmesan. Sprinkle the breadcrumb mixture evenly over the tomatoes. Bake for 10 minutes, or until the breadcrumbs are browned. Lay a sheet of foil over the tomatoes and bake for 10 minutes longer, or until the tomatoes are softened and heated through.

Preparation time 5 minutes • **Total time** 30 minutes • **Per serving** 57 calories, 2 g. fat (33% of calories), 0.4 g. saturated fat, 1 mg. cholesterol, 199 mg. sodium, 1.8 g. dietary fiber, 40 mg. calcium, 1 mg. iron, 25 mg. vitamin C, 0.5 mg. beta-carotene • **Serves 4**

FOODWAYS

It's hard to imagine Italian food without tomatoes. However, as strongly as tomatoes are identified with Italian cuisine, they are New World natives and were not introduced to Italy until the 16th century. These first tomatoes were small and yellow, hence the Italian word for tomatoes—*pomodori,* or golden apples. By the 18th century larger red tomatoes had been bred and were beginning to be popular as a salad ingredient; only later did people begin to cook them. Today, tomatoes are grown all over Italy, but the best plum tomatoes—most of which go into cans—come from San Marzano.

BRAISED GREENS WITH BEANS

3 garlic cloves, crushed

1 teaspoon extra-virgin olive oil

3 cups torn escarole, rinsed

4 cups trimmed, loosely packed fresh spinach

1 bunch watercress, tough stems removed

1 can (19 ounces) red kidney beans, rinsed and drained

1 teaspoon balsamic vinegar

¼ teaspoon sugar

¼ teaspoon salt

⅛ teaspoon freshly ground black pepper

This hearty accompaniment for a light meal brings together three types of greens with meaty red kidney beans in garlicky olive oil; balsamic vinegar and a touch of sugar are added later to make a mild sweet-and-sour sauce. In Italy, many vegetables are cooked in olive oil with garlic. While sturdy vegetables like broccoli are usually blanched first, greens such as escarole, spinach and watercress, used here, can go right into the skillet, where they'll wilt in a matter of minutes.

1 In a large, heavy saucepan, combine the garlic and oil. Cook over medium-high heat, stirring constantly, for 1 to 2 minutes, or until the garlic is fragrant.

2 Add the escarole, increase the heat to high and cook, stirring frequently, for 1 to 2 minutes, or until wilted. Add the spinach and watercress, and cook, stirring frequently, for 1 to 2 minutes, or until all the greens are wilted and tender.

3 Add the beans, vinegar, sugar, salt and black pepper. Reduce the heat to medium-low and stir to combine. Cover and cook for 5 minutes, or until the beans are heated through and the flavors are blended.

Preparation time 15 minutes • **Total time** 30 minutes • **Per serving** 139 calories, 2.3 g. fat (15% of calories), 0.3 g. saturated fat, 0 mg. cholesterol, 395 mg. sodium, 9.4 g. dietary fiber, 189 mg. calcium, 4 mg. iron, 46 mg. vitamin C, 5 mg. beta-carotene • **Serves 4**

MARKET AND PANTRY
Watercress is sold in fat little bunches, which are sometimes set in a tub of water to keep them fresh. Choose a bunch with crisp, dark green leaves and stems. For cooking, you need only cut off the tough bottom part of the stems; for salads, you just pinch off individual sprigs or leaves.

SOFT POLENTA WITH GORGONZOLA

3½ cups cold water

½ teaspoon salt

1 cup yellow cornmeal

¼ cup 1% low-fat milk

1 ounce Gorgonzola cheese without rind, crumbled

1 tablespoon plus 1 teaspoon Neufchâtel cream cheese

½ teaspoon chopped fresh thyme or 1 tablespoon chopped parsley

¼ teaspoon freshly ground black pepper

Polenta, a sort of mush or porridge made from meal, can be prepared with oats, spelt, barley, millet, chestnut flour or buckwheat, but today it is most commonly made from coarse-ground yellow cornmeal. Corn was a gift from the New World to Europe, and cornmeal polenta did not become popular in Italy until the 17th century. Creamy and bland, polenta needs a jolt of flavor that is often supplied by a sharp cheese, such as pungent Gorgonzola.

1 In a large, heavy no-stick saucepan, combine the water and salt, and bring to a boil over high heat. Whisking constantly, add the cornmeal in a slow, steady stream.

2 Reduce the heat to medium-low and cook the cornmeal mixture, stirring frequently and vigorously with a wooden spoon, for 15 minutes, or until the cornmeal is thickened, glossy and very smooth. Stir in the milk and remove the pan from the heat.

3 Stir in the Gorgonzola and Neufchâtel, the thyme or parsley and the black pepper. Stir until the cheeses are melted. Serve immediately.

Preparation time 10 minutes • **Total time** 35 minutes • **Per serving** 171 calories, 4.1 g. fat (21% of calories), 2.3 g. saturated fat, 10 mg. cholesterol, 399 mg. sodium, 1.9 g. dietary fiber, 65 mg. calcium, 2 mg. iron, 1 mg. vitamin C, 0.2 mg. beta-carotene • **Serves 4**

Gorgonzola, which originated near Milan, has a powerful flavor. One ounce is sufficient to flavor a big pot of polenta.

American Neufchâtel is a reduced-fat cream cheese. It gives the polenta a rich texture without adding a lot of fat.

ROASTED ASPARAGUS WITH GREEN SAUCE

1 **pound fresh asparagus spears, trimmed**

1 **teaspoon grated lemon zest**

1 **teaspoon extra-virgin olive oil**

¼ **teaspoon salt**

¼ **teaspoon freshly ground black pepper**

⅓ **cup packed Italian parsley sprigs**

⅓ **cup sliced scallions**

2 **tablespoons defatted chicken broth**

2 **garlic cloves, sliced**

½ **teaspoon dried tarragon, crumbled**

⅔ **cup plain nonfat yogurt**

1 **tablespoon fresh lemon juice**

1 **tablespoon low-fat mayonnaise**

Lemon wedges (optional)

Asparagus has been grown in Italy since Roman times; the asparagus grown in Ravenna, in the Emilia-Romagna region, was praised by the ancients, including famed historian Pliny the Elder. Here is a pleasing way to present the succulent spears (which may be served hot, warm or chilled): with a creamy lemon-herb sauce. Roasting, an unusual method for green vegetables, cooks the asparagus slowly and evenly. Note that the cooking time will depend on the thickness (or thinness) of the asparagus stalks.

1 Preheat the oven to 425°. Spray an 11 x 7-inch baking dish with no-stick spray.

2 Arrange the asparagus in the prepared pan. Sprinkle with the lemon zest, then drizzle with the oil. Sprinkle with ⅛ teaspoon each of the salt and black pepper. Turn the asparagus to coat it with the seasonings. Bake, turning the asparagus a few times, for 20 to 25 minutes, or until the spears are tender.

3 Meanwhile, in a small skillet, combine the parsley, scallions, broth, garlic and tarragon. Bring to a boil over high heat, then cover and simmer, stirring occasionally, for 3 to 4 minutes, or until the scallions are tender.

4 Transfer the mixture to a food processor. Add the yogurt, lemon juice, mayonnaise and the remaining ⅛ teaspoon each salt and black pepper, and purée until smooth. Transfer to a small bowl.

5 Serve the asparagus with the green sauce on the side. Offer lemon wedges, if desired.

Preparation time 15 minutes • **Total time** 30 minutes • **Per serving** 71 calories, 2 g. fat (26% of calories), 0.2 g. saturated fat, 1 mg. cholesterol, 238 mg. sodium, 1.6 g. dietary fiber, 122 mg. calcium, 1 mg. iron, 44 mg. vitamin C, 0.8 mg. beta-carotene • **Serves 4**

MAPLE CARROTS

8 large carrots, cut into thin diagonal slices

1 tablespoon pure maple syrup

2 teaspoons unsalted butter or margarine

Large pinch of ground cinnamon

Pinch of ground ginger

1 tablespoon chopped fresh cilantro (optional)

Carrots are among the most popular vegetables in America, and it's fortunate that they are so well-liked: A super source of beta-carotene, carrots also provide good amounts of potassium and both soluble and insoluble fiber. Keep carrot sticks on hand for snacks, add grated carrots to salads and sandwiches and, for a change, serve steamed carrot slices, glazed with maple syrup and butter, as an appetizing addition to a simple dinner. Instead of slicing the carrots, you might like to try roll-cutting them (see below).

1 In a deep, medium skillet, bring ½ inch of water to a boil over high heat. Add the carrots and return to a boil. Reduce the heat to medium and simmer for 5 to 6 minutes, or until the carrots are tender. Drain the carrots in a colander; dry the skillet.

2 Add the maple syrup, butter or margarine, cinnamon and ginger to the skillet, and return to medium heat. Cook, stirring constantly, until the butter melts and bubbles. Add the carrots and the cilantro, if using, and toss until the carrots are glazed and heated through.

Preparation time 10 minutes • **Total time** 10 minutes • **Per serving** 66 calories, 2.1 g. fat (28% of calories), 1.2 g. saturated fat, 5 mg. cholesterol, 30 mg. sodium, 2.6 g. dietary fiber, 27 mg. calcium, 1 mg. iron, 8 mg. vitamin C, 14 mg. beta-carotene
Serves 4

❧ ❧ ❧

To roll-cut carrots, first cut off the end of a carrot on a sharp diagonal.

Keeping the knife at the same angle, roll the carrot 180° and make a second cut.

BUTTERMILK MASHED POTATOES

1 pound baking potatoes, such as russets, peeled and cut into 1-inch chunks

1 cup water

½ cup defatted chicken broth

2 garlic cloves, unpeeled

¼ cup low-fat buttermilk

2 tablespoons thinly sliced scallions

⅛ teaspoon freshly ground pepper, preferably white

Large pinch of salt

Mashed potatoes give meals the comforting taste of home. Traditionally, the potatoes would be finished with butter and cream, but there are other ways to add richness: For this recipe, the potatoes are cooked in broth with garlic cloves, then mashed with buttermilk and sliced scallions. Mash the potatoes smooth, or leave them truly "homestyle"—a bit lumpy.

1 In a medium saucepan, combine the potatoes, water, broth and garlic cloves. Cover and bring to a boil over high heat. Reduce the heat to medium-low and simmer for 12 to 15 minutes, or until the potatoes are fork-tender.

2 Just before the potatoes are done, place the buttermilk in a small, heavy saucepan and warm it over low heat.

3 Drain the potatoes well; discard the garlic cloves. Return the potatoes to the pan and mash them with a potato masher.

4 Stir the warmed buttermilk, scallions, ground pepper and salt into the potatoes and serve.

Preparation time 10 minutes • **Total time** 30 minutes • **Per serving** 96 calories, 0.5 g. fat (5% of calories), 0.1 g. saturated fat, 1 mg. cholesterol, 191 mg. sodium, 1.8 g. dietary fiber, 24 mg. calcium, 1 mg. iron, 17 mg. vitamin C, 0 mg. beta-carotene
Serves 4

This type of potato masher requires a fair amount of pressure.

The more open wire masher is a little easier to use because there's less resistance.

An electric mixer on low speed is the easiest way to mash potatoes.

BROCCOLI WITH CORN AND CRISP GARLIC

1 lemon

3 cups small broccoli florets

¾ cup frozen corn kernels

1 teaspoon extra-virgin olive oil

3 garlic cloves, thinly sliced

¼ teaspoon freshly ground black
pepper

⅛ teaspoon salt

As readily available as broccoli is today, it wasn't until the mid-20th century that this vegetable gained popularity in the United States. In Italy, where broccoli has been a mainstay for centuries, it is often dressed, as it is here, with garlicky oil.

1 Using a swivel-bladed vegetable peeler, remove 2 or 3 wide bands of zest from the lemon; cut enough zest into thin strips to measure a scant tablespoon. Squeeze 1 tablespoon of juice from the lemon.

2 In a covered, deep medium skillet, bring ½ inch of water to a boil over high heat. Add the broccoli and return to a boil. Cook, turning the pieces occasionally, for 3 to 4 minutes, or until the broccoli is crisp-tender. Add the corn during the last minute or so of cooking time. Drain the broccoli and corn in a colander, and transfer to a heated platter; cover and keep warm.

3 In a small skillet, warm the oil over medium heat. Add the garlic, black pepper and salt, and sauté, stirring constantly, for about 1 minute, or until the garlic just begins to brown. Add the lemon zest and lemon juice, and stir to combine; immediately pour the garlic mixture over the broccoli and corn.

Preparation time 10 minutes • **Total time** 25 minutes • **Per serving** 72 calories, 1.7 g. fat (21% of calories), 0.2 g. saturated fat, 0 mg. cholesterol, 94 mg. sodium, 4 g. dietary fiber, 49 mg. calcium, 1 mg. iron, 0 mg. vitamin C, 1 mg. beta-carotene
Serves 4

❧ ❧ ❧

First, shave wide strips of peel from the lemon, removing only the colored zest.

Then, with a sharp paring knife, cut each piece of lemon zest into thin strips.

MASHED SWEET POTATOES WITH HONEY

1 **pound sweet potatoes, peeled
and cut into 1-inch chunks**

¼ **cup apricot nectar**

1 **tablespoon honey**

⅛ **teaspoon ground cinnamon**

**Large pinch of freshly ground
black pepper**

It seems a pity to serve sweet potatoes only during the holidays—
and it's practically a crime to bury their velvety texture and wonderful natural sweetness under a layer of marshmallows and
brown sugar. This notably nutritious vegetable, available all year round
in most supermarkets, can be boiled, steamed, baked, roasted or even
grilled. Bring out the sweet potato's savory side with the same toppings
you'd use for white potatoes—such as yogurt and chives—or enhance
its sweetness with a touch of honey and some apricot nectar.

1 Place the sweet potatoes in a medium saucepan and add enough
cold water to cover them. Cover the pan and bring to a boil over high
heat. Reduce the heat to medium-low and simmer for 12 to 15 minutes, or until the potatoes are fork-tender.

2 Meanwhile, in a small saucepan, warm the apricot nectar over
medium-low heat.

3 Drain the potatoes in a colander and return them to the saucepan in
which they were cooked. Add the apricot nectar, honey, cinnamon
and black pepper, and mash until smooth.

Preparation time 10 minutes • **Total time** 35 minutes • **Per serving** 111 calories,
0.3 g. fat (2% of calories), 0 g. saturated fat, 0 mg. cholesterol, 11 mg. sodium,
0.5 g. dietary fiber, 20 mg. calcium, 1 mg. iron, 27 mg. vitamin C, 10 mg. beta-
carotene • **Serves 4**

MARKET AND PANTRY
Although sweet potatoes look quite sturdy,
they are highly susceptible to decay. Buy
potatoes that are smooth, firm and free
of shriveled or dark areas. Store them in a
cool, dry place (about 55° is best), not in
the refrigerator, where their natural sug-
ars will turn to starch, robbing the potatoes
of their unique flavor.

FOR A CHANGE
Season the mashed sweet potatoes with
nutmeg, allspice, ginger or cloves.

ON THE MENU
These lightly sweet and spicy potatoes
are delicious with pork or poultry. For a
holiday meal, offer both mashed sweet
and white potatoes.

TOMATO AND CORN SUCCOTASH

1 cup trimmed, halved green beans

1 teaspoon olive oil

1 medium onion, chopped

1 garlic clove, minced

¼ teaspoon dried thyme, crumbled

⅛ teaspoon freshly ground black pepper

⅛ teaspoon salt

Large pinch of sugar

2 tablespoons defatted chicken broth or water

2 small ripe tomatoes, coarsely chopped

1 cup fresh or frozen corn kernels

As prepared in colonial America, succotash was a simple stew of corn and lima beans, enriched with salt pork and milk. The dish evolved in time, with the addition of other seasonal ingredients—such as bell peppers and tomatoes—and creative seasonings. For this colorful rendition, fresh corn is combined with green beans and tomatoes; the flavor is accentuated with onions, garlic and thyme.

1 In a deep medium skillet, bring ½ inch of water to a boil over high heat. Add the green beans and return to a boil. Cook for 3 to 5 minutes, stirring occasionally, until the beans are crisp-tender. Drain the beans in a colander; dry the skillet.

2 Add the oil to the same skillet, then stir in the onions, garlic, thyme, black pepper, salt and sugar. Sauté over medium-high heat for 1 minute, then stir in 1 tablespoon of the broth or water and sauté for 4 to 5 minutes, or until the onions are tender.

3 Stir in the blanched green beans, the tomatoes, corn and the remaining 1 tablespoon broth or water, and bring to a simmer. Reduce the heat to medium-low, cover and simmer, stirring occasionally, for 5 minutes, or until the tomatoes release their juices and all the vegetables are tender.

Preparation time 10 minutes • **Total time** 35 minutes • **Per serving** 81 calories, 1.9 g. fat (21% of calories), 0.2 g. saturated fat, 0 mg. cholesterol, 114 mg. sodium, 3.1 g. dietary fiber, 26 mg. calcium, 1 mg. iron, 20 mg. vitamin C, 0.4 mg. beta-carotene • **Serves 4**

MARKET AND PANTRY
Corn loses its natural sweetness very quickly after it's picked. Short of growing your own corn, the best guarantee of freshness is to buy corn at the farm where it is harvested, or at a farmer's market.

KITCHEN TIP
You can buy a special cutter to remove the kernels from fresh corn: This metal trough, about the size of an ear of corn, has a center opening fitted with blades. When you slide an ear of corn across the blades, they cut off the kernels, which drop through the opening. It's easy to cut the kernels from corn with a knife, too. Trim one end of an ear of corn so that you can stand it upright on a cutting board. Slide the blade of a sharp knife down the ear to cut off the kernels. Press gently so that you don't cut off any of the fibrous cob along with the tender kernels.

SPINACH WITH MUSHROOMS

2 large shallots or 1 small onion, chopped

¼ cup defatted chicken broth or water

¾ teaspoon olive oil

4 ounces small fresh mushrooms, quartered

1 pound washed spinach, tough stems removed

⅛ teaspoon salt

⅛ teaspoon freshly ground black pepper

We've come a long way since the time when cookbooks directed that spinach and other tender greens be "stewed" for half an hour, turning them into a gray mush with little nutritional value. When spinach is cooked just long enough to wilt it, the leaves stay a vibrant green and little of the vitamin C is lost.

1 In a large no-stick skillet, combine the shallots or onions, 2 tablespoons of the broth or water and the oil. Place the skillet over medium-high heat and cook, stirring constantly, for 3 to 4 minutes, or until the shallots or onions are tender.

2 Add the mushrooms and the remaining 2 tablespoons broth or water, and cook, stirring frequently, for 4 to 6 minutes, or until the mushrooms are tender.

3 Increase the heat to high. Add the spinach by handfuls and stir constantly until the spinach wilts; cook for 1 minute longer, season with the salt and pepper, and serve.

Preparation time 15 minutes • **Total time** 25 minutes • **Per serving** 39 calories, 1.3 g. fat (30% of calories), 0.2 g. saturated fat, 0 mg. cholesterol, 197 mg. sodium, 2.5 g. dietary fiber, 86 mg. calcium, 3 mg. iron, 24 mg. vitamin C, 3 mg. beta-carotene
Serves 4

Wash the spinach and gently pat it dry with a kitchen towel.

Hold the leaves between your fingers and pull off the stem from each leaf.

PART 6
Desserts

GINGERED CANTALOUPE SORBET

1 large ripe cantaloupe, peeled,
  seeded and cut into chunks
  (about 4 cups)

½ cup sugar

2 tablespoons light corn syrup

1 tablespoon fresh lemon juice

1 tablespoon peeled grated fresh
  ginger

2 tablespoons minced crystallized
  ginger

  Mint sprigs, for garnish
  (optional)

Fine-quality crystallized ginger comes in
good-size chunks and slices.

You don't need an ice-cream machine to make sorbet—just a
food processor—and you can produce flavors you'll never
find at the supermarket, like this sublime gingered melon ice.
It contains both pungent fresh ginger and sweet-hot crystallized ginger—lively accents to the fragrant sweetness of the melon.

1 Place the cantaloupe, sugar, corn syrup, lemon juice and fresh ginger in a food processor, and process until smooth. Add the crystallized ginger and pulse just until mixed. Pour into a 9 x 9-inch metal
baking pan, cover with foil and freeze for at least 6 hours, or overnight,
or until frozen hard.

2 Remove the sorbet from the freezer and let stand for a few minutes
until softened. Break the sorbet into chunks. In batches, place the
sorbet in a food processor and pulse until creamy and smooth.

3 Transfer the sorbet to a freezer container, cover and freeze for at
least 1 hour, or until you are ready to serve.

4 To serve, soften at room temperature for a few minutes. Spoon
the sorbet into 4 dessert dishes or goblets. Garnish with mint sprigs, if
desired.

Preparation time 10 minutes • **Total time** 20 minutes plus chilling time • **Per
serving** 211 calories, 0.5 g. fat (2% of calories), 0 g. saturated fat, 0 mg. cholesterol,
32 mg. sodium, 1.3 g. dietary fiber, 37 mg. calcium, 2 mg. iron, 73 mg. vitamin C,
3.1 mg. beta-carotene • **Serves 4**

MARKET AND PANTRY
Crystallized ginger is made by cooking
slices of fresh ginger in a sugar syrup,
then coating it with granulated sugar. This
turns the ginger into a tasty confection
with a consistency like that of firm dried
fruit. The crystallized ginger sold in small
jars in supermarket spice racks can be
very expensive. Better bets are gourmet or
candy shops, or Asian markets, where the
ginger is sold by the pound. It's usually
much cheaper and also of better quality.

FRESH FRUIT TERRINE

1 envelope plus 1 teaspoon
  unflavored gelatin

½ cup cold water

2 cups cranberry juice cocktail

3 tablespoons sugar

3 medium nectarines, cut into thin
  wedges (about 3 cups)

1¾ cups sliced fresh strawberries

Nectarine slices and halved
strawberries, for garnish
(optional)

For smooth slices, use a thin serrated knife
and dip the blade into hot water before
making each cut.

There's just no comparison, in terms of flavor, between this "stained-glass" dessert and one made from a boxed dessert mix. However, the method and preparation time are pretty much the same, so why not start from scratch? The slices of nectarine and berries are so pretty that you don't need to use a fancy mold—a simple loaf pan will do. This gives the dessert the shape of a classic French *terrine,* and makes turning it out of the mold easier, too.

1 Spray an 8 x 4-inch loaf pan with no-stick spray.

2 In a medium metal bowl, sprinkle the gelatin over the cold water and let stand for 2 minutes to soften.

3 In a small saucepan, combine the cranberry juice cocktail and sugar, and bring to a boil over high heat, stirring to dissolve the sugar. Pour the boiling juice mixture over the softened gelatin and stir until the gelatin is completely dissolved.

4 Place the bowl with the cranberry-gelatin mixture over a larger bowl of ice water and let sit, stirring occasionally, for 8 to 10 minutes, or until the mixture is cold and just starts to jell. Stir in the fruits and turn the mixture into the prepared loaf pan. Cover with plastic wrap and chill for at least 6 hours, or overnight, until set.

5 To unmold, dip the pan briefly into a basin of hot water and invert over a platter. Shake to loosen the terrine, then remove the pan.

6 If desired, surround the terrine with nectarine slices and halved strawberries, or cut the terrine into 8 slices, place a slice on each of 8 dessert plates and garnish each serving with the fresh fruits.

Preparation time 10 minutes • **Total time** 30 minutes plus chilling time • **Per serving** 94 calories, 0.5 g. fat (5% of calories), 0 g. saturated fat, 0 mg. cholesterol, 4 mg. sodium, 1.7 g. dietary fiber, 10 mg. calcium, 0 mg. iron, 44 mg. vitamin C, 0.2 mg. beta-carotene • **Serves 8**

CREAMY BANANA PUDDING

¾ **cup sweetened condensed milk**

1 **tablespoon plus 1 teaspoon fresh lemon juice**

2 **cups vanilla nonfat yogurt**

½ **cup reduced-fat sour cream**

1 **teaspoon vanilla extract**

⅓ **cup cold water**

1 **envelope unflavored gelatin**

4 **large bananas**

20 **reduced-fat vanilla wafers**

One of the South's most beloved desserts, this family-pleaser depends for its flavor on sweet, ripe bananas. Some of the other ingredients in this version, however, are not traditional. Instead of whole milk, butter, eggs and heavy cream, the pudding is made with vanilla nonfat yogurt and reduced-fat sour cream. Gelatin, rather than cornstarch, serves as a thickener.

1 In a medium bowl, whisk the condensed milk with 1 tablespoon of the lemon juice until slightly thickened. Whisk in the yogurt, sour cream and vanilla until smooth.

2 Pour the cold water into a small saucepan. Sprinkle the gelatin over the water and let soften for 2 minutes. Cook the gelatin mixture over medium heat, stirring constantly, for 1 to 2 minutes, or until the gelatin is completely dissolved and the mixture is heated through. Stir the dissolved gelatin into the yogurt mixture.

3 Slice 3 of the bananas into ¼-inch-thick rounds. Drizzle with the remaining 1 teaspoon lemon juice. Fold the bananas into the pudding. Pour the pudding into 8 dessert glasses or a serving bowl, cover and chill for at least 2 hours, or until the pudding is set but still has a soft texture.

4 Just before serving, slice the remaining banana into ¼-inch-thick slices. Arrange the banana slices and the vanilla wafers on top of the pudding. To soften the cookies, let the pudding stand for a few minutes before serving.

Preparation time 5 minutes • **Total time** 25 minutes plus chilling time • **Per serving** 273 calories, 5.9 g. fat (19% of calories), 2.8 g. saturated fat, 16 mg. cholesterol, 131 mg. sodium, 1.2 g. dietary fiber, 169 mg. calcium, 1 mg. iron, 8 mg. vitamin C, 0.1 mg. beta-carotene • **Serves 8**

SUBSTITUTION
If you can't get reduced-fat vanilla wafers, you can use the regular kind and still end up with a healthful dessert: Even the regular wafers are relatively low in fat. Eight of them have 5.1 grams of fat, while the same quantity of reduced-fat wafers have 3.5 grams of fat.

SPICED PLUMS WITH CHANTILLY SAUCE

¾ **cup plain nonfat yogurt**

1 **pound ripe prune plums or black plums**

⅓ **cup purple grape juice**

3 **tablespoons Damson plum preserves**

1 **tablespoon sugar**

⅛ **teaspoon ground allspice**

Two 2-inch-long strips lemon zest

Half a cinnamon stick or a large pinch of ground cinnamon

2 **tablespoons reduced-fat sour cream**

2 **tablespoons confectioners' sugar**

1 **vanilla bean or ½ teaspoon vanilla extract**

The gracefully named *crème Chantilly*, a classic French dessert topping, consists of sweetened whipped heavy cream flavored with a touch of vanilla or a liqueur, such as chocolate *crème de cacao* or cherry-flavored *kirsch*. Here, yogurt cream, made by draining the whey from yogurt, takes the place of the whipped cream. Using a vanilla bean rather than extract gives the sauce a richer flavor.

1 Line a strainer with cheesecloth or a double layer of paper towels and place the strainer over a medium bowl. Spoon the yogurt into the strainer and let drain for 30 minutes. Discard the whey, wipe out the bowl and spoon the yogurt into the bowl; set aside.

2 While the yogurt is draining, halve and pit the plums. If using black plums, cut them into quarters.

3 In a medium, heavy nonreactive saucepan, combine the grape juice, preserves, sugar and allspice, and stir well. Add the plums, lemon zest and cinnamon stick or ground cinnamon, and stir to combine.

4 Bring the plum mixture to a boil over medium-high heat. Reduce the heat to medium-low, cover and simmer, stirring occasionally, for 5 to 10 minutes, or until the plums are tender but not mushy. Pour the plums and syrup into a medium bowl, cover with vented plastic wrap and refrigerate for about 1 hour, or until chilled.

5 Meanwhile, make the Chantilly sauce. Whisk the sour cream and confectioners' sugar into the drained yogurt. If using the vanilla bean, cut the bean in half lengthwise and scrape the seeds into the yogurt; whisk to blend. Or, if using the vanilla extract, add to the yogurt and whisk to blend.

6 Discard the cinnamon stick, if using, then spoon the plums and syrup into 4 dessert dishes. Top each serving with 2 heaping tablespoons of the Chantilly sauce.

Halve the vanilla bean lengthwise, then scrape out the seeds. Save the vanilla bean halves and bury them in sugar to make vanilla sugar.

Preparation time 10 minutes • **Total time** 35 minutes plus chilling time • **Per serving** 163 calories, 1.7 g. fat (9% of calories), 0.6 g. saturated fat, 3 mg. cholesterol, 26 mg. sodium, 2.4 g. dietary fiber, 64 mg. calcium, 0 mg. iron, 17 mg. vitamin C, 0.2 mg. beta-carotene • **Serves 4**

Amaretti Pudding

2 cups 1% low-fat milk

⅓ cup packed light brown sugar

¼ cup cornstarch

¼ teaspoon salt

½ cup skim milk

1 teaspoon vanilla extract

5 large amaretti cookies
(1¼ ounces), crumbled

Velvety desserts like this vanilla pudding need something crunchy for contrast. Here, crumbled *amaretti*—crisp almond-flavored macaroons from Italy—top the pudding. You can find amaretti, in brightly colored tins or bags, at gourmet shops, Italian grocery stores and many supermarkets. If you can't buy them, however, try another crisp topping, such as crumbled chocolate or vanilla wafers, your favorite breakfast cereal or a few spoonfuls of toasted coconut.

1 In a medium, heavy saucepan, warm the low-fat milk over medium heat just until small bubbles form around the edge and the milk is steaming. Remove the pan from the heat and set aside.

2 Meanwhile, in a medium bowl, whisk together the sugar, cornstarch and salt until blended. (You may need to break up the lumps of sugar with your fingers.) Gradually whisk in the skim milk until the mixture is smooth.

3 Pour the reserved low-fat milk into the sugar mixture and whisk until blended. Return the mixture to the saucepan and bring to a boil over medium heat, stirring constantly. Continue to boil, stirring, for 1 minute. Remove from the heat and stir in the vanilla.

4 Ladle the pudding into 4 dessert dishes or glasses, cover and refrigerate for about 1½ hours, or until chilled.

5 Just before serving, sprinkle each pudding with some amaretti crumbs.

Preparation time 10 minutes • **Total time** 30 minutes plus chilling time • **Per serving** 203 calories, 2.3 g. fat (10% of calories), 0.8 g. saturated fat, 6 mg. cholesterol, 224 mg. sodium, 0.1 g. dietary fiber, 204 mg. calcium, 0 mg. iron, 2 mg. vitamin C, 0.2 mg. beta-carotene • **Serves 4**

KITCHEN TIP
As anyone who's ever made gravy knows, cornstarch sometimes forms lumps when stirred into liquid. Combining the cornstarch with the sugar, and then whisking in the milk, helps keep this from happening.

MARGARITA FRUITS

3 cups whole strawberries, hulled
and quartered

2 tablespoons granulated sugar

2 tablespoons frozen orange juice
concentrate

½ teaspoon grated lime zest

2 tablespoons fresh lime juice

1 tablespoon tequila (optional)

3 cups honeydew balls

Lime wedges, raw sugar and
grated lime zest, for garnish
(optional)

The Mexican cocktail called a *margarita* is made from tequila, orange liqueur and lime juice—a potent mixture that belies its innocent name (*margarita* is Spanish for "daisy"). To provide a sharp foil for its fruitiness, the drink is often served in a glass edged with coarse salt. Here, the dessert goblets are edged with raw sugar, available in most supermarkets.

1 In a medium bowl, combine the strawberries and granulated sugar. Let stand for 25 minutes, or until the juices begin to flow.

2 In a small bowl, combine the orange juice concentrate, lime zest, lime juice, and tequila, if using. Add the strawberries and their juice and the honeydew balls, and mix gently with a rubber spatula.

3 If desired, for a traditional margarita presentation, moisten the rims of 4 goblets with lime wedges. Place the raw sugar on a plate and dip the rim of each goblet into the sugar to coat it.

4 Carefully spoon the fruits and juice into the goblets and garnish each serving with lime zest, if desired.

Preparation time 10 minutes • **Total time** 25 minutes • **Per serving** 119 calories, 0.6 g. fat (4% of calories), 0 g. saturated fat, 0 mg. cholesterol, 14 mg. sodium, 4.2 g. dietary fiber, 28 mg. calcium, 1 mg. iron, 111 mg. vitamin C, 0.1 mg. beta-carotene • **Serves 4**

Scoop out the seeds and fibers from the honeydew with a tablespoon.

Then insert a melon baller deep into the flesh to make balls that are nearly round.

LEMON-MINT WATERMELON GRANITA

3 pounds watermelon, seeded and cut into chunks (about 4 cups)

⅓ cup sugar

⅓ cup fresh lemon juice

2 tablespoons light corn syrup

2 tablespoons slivered mint leaves

¾ teaspoon grated lemon zest

Even colder than a well-chilled watermelon, this refreshing dessert takes the form of a *granita,* a super-crunchy Italian ice. To produce the pleasantly granular texture, periodically stir and scrape the partially frozen mixture with a fork. This technique brings the iciest portions into the less-frozen center and maintains the crystalline quality of the ice.

1 Place the watermelon chunks, sugar, lemon juice and corn syrup in a blender or food processor, in batches if necessary, and process to a smooth purée. Add the slivered mint and lemon zest, and pulse just to mix.

2 Pour the watermelon mixture into a 9-inch square metal baking pan and place in the freezer. Freeze, scraping the frozen edges toward the middle every 30 minutes or so, for 2 to 3 hours, or until the granita is slushy and granular.

3 Cover and freeze for at least 2 to 3 hours longer, or until frozen hard.

4 To serve, scrape the surface of the ice with a metal spoon to create a granular texture, then spoon into 4 goblets or dessert dishes.

Preparation time 15 minutes • **Total time** 25 minutes plus chilling time • **Per serving** 150 calories, 0.7 g. fat (4% of calories), 0 g. saturated fat, 0 mg. cholesterol, 16 mg. sodium, 0.6 g. dietary fiber, 16 mg. calcium, 0 mg. iron, 26 mg. vitamin C, 0.4 mg. beta-carotene • **Serves 4**

MARKET AND PANTRY
You'll find two types of watermelon in the market, at least during the summer: picnic and icebox. Picnic watermelons weigh up to 50 pounds—they're the massive blimp-shaped fruits you'd serve at a barbecue.

Icebox melons are bred to fit into the refrigerator: They're round or oval and weigh from 5 to 10 pounds. Some icebox watermelons are seedless. With its deep-colored, crunchy flesh, a seedless melon would be ideal for this recipe.

SUMMER FRUITS WITH SPICED YOGURT

1½ **cups plain nonfat yogurt**

½ **medium cantaloupe**

2 **large nectarines**

3 **large plums**

½ **cup halved red seedless grapes**

2 **tablespoons honey**

⅛ **teaspoon ground cardamom**

8 **drops rosewater or almond extract**

After spooning the yogurt into the cheese-cloth-lined strainer, stir the yogurt to break it up a bit and start the whey separating.

The delicate fragrance of the yogurt sauce may be familiar to lovers of Indian cuisine. The thickened yogurt is blended with cardamom and rosewater, two ingredients featured in many Indian sweets: Whole cardamom pods or ground cardamom seeds flavor coconut pudding and coconut fudge as well as hot tea, and rosewater lends a delicate perfume to rice pudding, cashew fudge and *lassi*—a yogurt "milkshake."

1 Line a strainer with cheesecloth or a double layer of paper towels and place the strainer over a medium bowl. Spoon the yogurt into the strainer and let drain for 20 minutes. Discard the whey, wipe out the bowl and spoon the yogurt into the bowl.

2 While the yogurt is draining, peel and seed the cantaloupe, and cut it into bite-size chunks. Place the cantaloupe in a medium serving bowl. Slice the nectarines and plums, and add to the cantaloupe. Add the grapes and stir to combine.

3 Add the honey, cardamom and rosewater or almond extract to the drained yogurt, and whisk to blend.

4 Drizzle the fruits with some of the spiced yogurt and serve the rest of the yogurt on the side.

Preparation time 5 minutes • **Total time** 30 minutes • **Per serving** 116 calories, 0.7 g. fat (5% of calories), 0 g. saturated fat, 0 mg. cholesterol, 24 mg. sodium, 2.3 g. dietary fiber, 81 mg. calcium, 0 mg. iron, 25 mg. vitamin C, 1.1 mg. beta-carotene • **Serves 6**

MARKET AND PANTRY
Rosewater is made from roses specially grown for their fragrance. It is sold in gourmet shops, Middle Eastern stores and many pharmacies.

SUBSTITUTION
If you're unable to get rosewater, or don't care for it, use almond extract instead. Be sure to buy pure almond extract—the imitation type has a distinctly inferior flavor.

Warm Gingerbread-Pumpkin Pudding

2 large eggs

2 large egg whites

¼ cup mild molasses

¼ cup sugar

1 cup solid-pack canned pumpkin

¾ cup skim milk

⅓ cup all-purpose flour

2 teaspoons ground ginger

1½ teaspoons ground cinnamon

1 teaspoon baking powder

½ teaspoon baking soda

¼ teaspoon ground allspice

⅛ teaspoon ground white pepper

1 teaspoon confectioners' sugar

Recipes for the steamed holiday puddings of Dickens's day make wonderful reading, but they required no end of time and effort, what with chopping the fruits, nuts and suet, mixing the batter in a mammoth bowl, steaming it in a cloth-wrapped basin for 9 to 12 hours and then aging the finished product for many months to blend the flavors to perfection. This spicy pumpkin pudding-cake—a flash in the pan by comparison—makes a terrific holiday dessert. Dress it up with a scoop of vanilla or lemon frozen yogurt.

1 Preheat the oven to 400°. Spray an 8- or 9-inch square baking dish with no-stick spray.

2 In a large bowl, combine the eggs, egg whites, molasses and sugar, and whisk until smooth. Whisk in the pumpkin and milk.

3 Add the flour, ginger, cinnamon, baking powder, baking soda, allspice and white pepper, and whisk just until smooth. Pour the batter into the prepared pan.

4 Bake for 25 minutes, or until the pudding is lightly browned and cracked around the edges but still a bit soft in the center. Transfer to a wire rack to cool briefly.

5 Just before serving, place the confectioners' sugar in a small strainer and dust over the warm pudding.

Preparation time 5 minutes • **Total time** 35 minutes • **Per serving** 156 calories, 2.1 g. fat (12% of calories), 0.6 g. saturated fat, 71 mg. cholesterol, 249 mg. sodium, 0.9 g. dietary fiber, 140 mg. calcium, 2 mg. iron, 2 mg. vitamin C, 5.5 mg. beta-carotene • **Serves 6**

KITCHEN TIP

White pepper might seem a bit out of place in the list of gingerbread spices, but it is actually a traditional ingredient in European recipes. Try a pinch of white pepper in your own recipes for ginger cookies or spice cakes.

MAKE AHEAD

Although this is a very quick recipe, you can shave off a few moments by measuring the dry ingredients in advance. Combine the flour, ginger, cinnamon, baking powder, baking soda, allspice and pepper in a container, stir well and cover.

BLONDIES

1 cup packed dark brown sugar

½ cup unsweetened applesauce

2 tablespoons butter, melted

1 large egg

1 large egg white

1½ teaspoons vanilla extract

1¾ cups all-purpose flour

2 teaspoons baking powder

½ teaspoon salt

¼ cup chopped walnuts

Brown sugar stored in the box often turns lumpy and hard. To avoid this, transfer the sugar to a jar and add a slice of apple or a piece of fresh bread.

Blondies are un-chocolate brownies; in fact, they were originally called blond brownies. They're rich, chewy bar cookies made with brown sugar for a butterscotchy flavor. Of course, you can't have butterscotch without butter, but this recipe calls for just 2 tablespoons: Applesauce takes the place of most of the shortening. Compare this with standard blondie recipes, which commonly use ½ to ¾ cup of butter.

1 Preheat the oven to 350°. Spray a 13 x 9-inch baking pan with no-stick spray.

2 In a large bowl, with an electric mixer at medium speed, beat the brown sugar, applesauce, butter, egg, egg white and vanilla until well combined.

3 With the mixer at low speed, beat in the flour, baking powder and salt. Stir in the nuts. Spread the mixture evenly in the prepared pan. Bake for 15 to 20 minutes, or until a toothpick inserted in the center comes out clean. Remove the pan to a wire rack to cool completely. Cut into 24 bars.

Preparation time 15 minutes • **Total time** 30 minutes • **Per bar** 92 calories, 2 g. fat (20% of calories), 0.7 g. saturated fat, 11 mg. cholesterol, 105 mg. sodium, 0.4 g. dietary fiber, 35 mg. calcium, 1 mg. iron, 0 mg. vitamin C, 0 mg. beta-carotene
Makes 24 bars

FOR A CHANGE
Leave out the walnuts and add ½ cup of sweetened flaked coconut to the batter; if you do so, you can also substitute ½ tea-spoon of almond extract for ½ teaspoon of the vanilla. Or, try ½ cup of semisweet or milk chocolate chips or butterscotch chips instead of the walnuts.

CHOCOLATE PEANUT BUTTER BALLS

1½ cups chocolate-wafer cookie crumbs (about twenty-five 2½-inch cookies, finely crushed)

1 cup plus 2 tablespoons sifted confectioners' sugar

⅓ cup honey

¼ cup plus 2 tablespoons reduced-fat creamy peanut butter

To make cookie crumbs without making a mess, place the chocolate wafers in a heavy-duty zip-seal bag and crush them with a rolling pin.

If you love to give homemade cookies as holiday gifts—but dread the thought of long hours of baking—here's your solution: Make a few batches of these no-bake peanut-butter-and-chocolate gems, which look like fancy chocolate truffles (but are far lower in fat), and pack them in pretty boxes.

1 In a large bowl, combine the cookie crumbs and 1 cup of the confectioners' sugar.

2 In a medium bowl, whisk together the honey and peanut butter until well combined. Add the honey mixture to the cookie crumb mixture and stir until well combined. (The mixture may be crumbly at this point.)

3 With your hands, shape the mixture into thirty-six 1-inch balls (the mixture should hold together as you shape it). Set the balls aside at room temperature until ready to serve or store them in an air-tight container at room temperature for 2 to 3 days. Just before serving, roll each ball in the remaining 2 tablespoons confectioners' sugar.

Preparation time 10 minutes • **Total time** 35 minutes • **Per ball** 56 calories, 1.6 g. fat (25% of calories), 0.3 g. saturated fat, 0 mg. cholesterol, 36 mg. sodium, 0.2 g. dietary fiber, 2 mg. calcium, 0 mg. iron, 0 mg. vitamin C, 0 mg. beta-carotene
Makes 3 dozen balls

KITCHEN TIP

For elegant gifts, pack the cookies as if they were fine chocolates: Fluted paper or foil candy cups are sold at cookware shops and baking-supply houses. You could also use the paper liners made for miniature muffin pans, which are available at most housewares stores and many supermarkets.

NUTRITION NOTE

Regular peanut butter, which consists mainly of ground peanuts, is a high-fat food. But reduced-fat peanut spreads, which incorporate lower-fat ingredients such as corn syrup solids and soy protein, offer a better option: They contain about 6 grams of fat per tablespoon, rather than the 8 grams in regular peanut butter.

ZUCCOTTO

1 container (32 ounces) vanilla
  low-fat yogurt

¼ cup blanched slivered almonds

  One (13.6-ounce) fat-free
  pound cake

3 tablespoons fresh orange juice

2 tablespoons sweet Marsala wine

½ cup confectioners' sugar

1 square (1 ounce) semisweet
  chocolate, finely chopped

1 envelope unflavored gelatin

¼ cup cold water

  Sliced strawberries, for topping
  (optional)

Arrange enough pieces of cake in the bowl
so they line it snugly. This layer of cake
will form the dome that holds the filling.

In Italian, *zuccotto* means "skullcap"; this impressive dessert was apparently named for its domed shape. Substitute orange juice for the Marsala if you prefer to omit the alcohol.

1 Line a strainer with a double layer of paper towels and place over a medium bowl. Spoon in the yogurt and let drain for 4 hours. Discard the whey and spoon the yogurt into the bowl; refrigerate until needed.

2 Preheat the oven to 350°. Place the almonds in a baking pan and toast for about 8 minutes, or until lightly browned. Chop the nuts.

3 Spray a deep 8-cup bowl with no-stick spray. Line the bowl with plastic wrap. Cut the pound cake into twenty ¼-inch-thick slices. Place one whole slice of cake in the center of the bottom of the bowl. Cut the remaining slices in half diagonally. Arrange enough cake triangles around the inside of the bowl to cover the bowl, overlapping to fit.

4 In a cup, combine the orange juice and Marsala. Brush the cake slices with some of the orange juice mixture; set the remainder aside.

5 Add the confectioners' sugar, chocolate and toasted almonds to the drained yogurt, stirring until well combined. In a small saucepan, sprinkle the gelatin over the cold water and let stand for 1 minute. Cook over low heat, stirring, for 2 to 3 minutes, or until the gelatin dissolves. Gradually whisk the gelatin mixture into the yogurt mixture, whisking constantly until it is completely incorporated.

6 Gently spoon the yogurt mixture into the bowl to cover the cake. Cover the yogurt mixture completely with the remaining cake slices. Brush the remaining orange juice mixture onto the cake slices. Cover with plastic wrap and chill for at least 3 hours, or overnight.

7 To serve, uncover and invert the zuccotto onto a platter. Remove the bowl and plastic wrap. Top with sliced strawberries, if desired.

Preparation time 5 minutes • **Total time** 35 minutes plus draining and chilling time
Per serving 183 calories, 3.4 g. fat (17% of calories), 0.6 g. saturated fat, 2 mg. cholesterol, 137 mg. sodium, 0.8 g. dietary fiber, 89 mg. calcium, 0 mg. iron, 2 mg. vitamin C, 0.1 mg. beta-carotene • **Serves 12**

INDEX

❧ ❧ ❧

Boldface page references indicate photographs.

Honeydew melon
  Margarita Fruits, **148**, 149

Indian-style dishes
  Bow-Ties with Curried Beef, **74**, 75
Italian-style dishes
  Chicken Mozzarella, 64, **65**
  Chicken Piccata with Escarole, **62**, 63
  Smoked Turkey Carbonara, 110, **111**
  Turkey Cutlets Milanese, **56**, 57
  Turkey Tetrazzini, 96, **97**
  Tuscan Pork with White Beans, 40, **41**
  Zuccoto, **160**, 161

Jalapeño chilies
  Mexican Taco Salad, **8**, 9
Jambalaya
  Seafood Jambalaya, 36, **37**
Japanese-style dishes
  Turkey Tonkatsu with Vegetables, 50, **51**

Kidney beans
  Braised Greens with Beans, **118**, 119
  Chicken Mozzarella, 64, **65**

Lamb
  Pasta with Lamb and Rosemary Pesto, **80**, 81
Leeks
  Hearty Chicken and Greens Soup, 12, **13**
Legumes. *See* Beans; Chick-peas; Kidney beans; Peas
Lemon
  Broccoli with Corn and Crisp Garlic, 128, **129**
  Lemon-Dill Shrimp Caesar, **10**, 11
  Lemony Asparagus and Pasta Salad, **82**, 83
  Pasta with Lamb and Rosemary Pesto, **80**, 81
  Shrimp with Lemon and Almonds, 32, **33**
Lemon-Dill Shrimp Caesar, **10**, 11
Lemon-Rosemary Chicken Breast, 54, **55**
Lemony Asparagus and Pasta Salad, **82**, 83
Lettuce
  Cobb Salad with Parmesan Dressing, 22, **23**
  Lemon-Dill Shrimp Caesar, **10**, 11
  Mexican Taco Salad, **8**, 9
  Thai Beef Salad, **14**, 15
Limes
  Crispy Chicken with Nectarine Salsa, **52**, 53
  Southwestern Chicken Sauté, **44**, 45
Linguine
  Linguine with Smoked Salmon, 104, **105**
  Pasta Salad with Chick-peas, **94**, 95

Pasta with Cauliflower and Cheddar, 84, **85**
Smoked Turkey Carbonara, 110, **111**
Linguine with Smoked Salmon, 104, **105**

Macaroni
  Chicken Mozzarella, 64, **65**
  Macaroni and Cheese Salad, 88, **89**
  Picnic Macaroni-Tuna Salad, **100**, 101
Macaroni and Cheese Salad, 88, **89**
Mangoes
  Thai Beef Salad, **14**, 15
  Tropical Chicken Salad, **20**, 21
Maple Carrots, 124, **125**
Maple syrup
  Maple Carrots, 124, **125**
  Margarita Fruits, **148**, 149
Marsala wine
  Turkey-Sage Cutlets with Mushrooms, 58, **59**
  Zuccotto, **160**, 161
Mashed Sweet Potatoes with Honey, **130**, 131
Meat. *See specific types*
Mediterranean Seashell Salad, **102**, 103
Mediterranean-style dishes. *See* Greek-style dishes
Mediterranean-Style Tuna and Pasta, 30, **31**
Mexican-style dishes
  Mexican Taco Salad, **8**, 9
Mexican Taco Salad, **8**, 9
Milk
  Amaretti Pudding, 146, **147**
  Buttermilk Mashed Potatoes, 126, **127**
  Cobb Salad with Parmesan Dressing, 22, **23**
  Creamy Banana Pudding, **142**, 143
  Lemon-Dill Shrimp Caesar, **10**, 11
  Pasta with Cauliflower and Cheddar, 84, **85**
  Smoked Turkey Carbonara, 110, **111**
  Turkey Tetrazzini, 96, **97**
  Warm Gingerbread-Pumpkin Pudding, 154, **155**
Mint
  Pasta Salad with Chick-peas, **94**, 95
  Thai Beef Salad, **14**, 15
Mozzarella cheese
  Chicken Mozzarella, 64, **65**
Mushrooms
  Asian Chicken Noodle Soup, 18, **19**
  Double Orange Beef with Vegetables, **28**, 29
  Lemon-Dill Shrimp Caesar, **10**, 11
  Spinach with Mushrooms, 134, **135**
  Turkey-Sage Cutlets with Mushrooms, 58, **59**
  Turkey Tetrazzini, 96, **97**
Mustard. *See* Dijon mustard

Nectarines
  Crispy Chicken with Nectarine Salsa, **52**, 53
  Fresh Fruit Terrine, **140**, 141
  Summer Fruits with Spiced Yogurt, 152, **153**
Noodles
  Asian Chicken Noodle Soup, 18, **19**
  Hearty Chicken and Greens Soup, 12, **13**
  Turkey Tetrazzini, 96, **97**
Nuts
  Blondies, **156**, 157
  Chicken Breasts with Pears, 60, **61**
  Shrimp with Lemon and Almonds, 32, **33**
  Thai Beef Salad, **14**, 15
  Tropical Chicken Salad, **20**, 21
  Zuccotto, **160**, 161

Onions
  Chicken Mozzarella, 64, **65**
  Five-Spice Chicken with Vegetables, 38, **39**
  Fruited Chicken and Couscous Salad, **24**, 25
  Hoisin Pork and Vegetables, 34, **35**
  Mediterranean Seashell Salad, **102**, 103
  Mexican Taco Salad, **8**, 9
  Pasta Salad with Chick-peas, **94**, 95
  Penne with Broccoli and Chick-peas, 86, **87**
  Picnic Macaroni-Tuna Salad, **100**, 101
  Seafood Jambalaya, 36, **37**
  Shrimp with Lemon and Almonds, 32, **33**
  Spinach with Mushrooms, 134, **135**
  Tomato and Corn Succotash, **132**, 133
  Turkey Cutlets Milanese, **56**, 57
Orange marmalade
  Double Orange Beef with Vegetables, **28**, 29
  Turkey with Cranberry-Orange Sauce, 70, **71**
Oranges
  Double Orange Beef with Vegetables, **28**, 29
  Fruited Chicken and Couscous Salad, **24**, 25
  Rosemary-Orange Chicken on Spinach, **48**, 49
  Scallop and Orange Toss, **16**, 17
  Turkey with Cranberry-Orange Sauce, 70, **71**
Orzo
  Five-Spice Chicken with Vegetables, 38, **39**
  Warm Chicken and Orzo Salad, **4**, 5

Papayas
  Thai Beef Salad, **14**, 15
  Tropical Chicken Salad, **20**, 21
Parmesan-Baked Plum Tomatoes, **116**, 117

Index • 167

International Conversion Chart

These equivalents have been slightly rounded to make measuring easier.

Volume Measurements

U.S.	Imperial	Metric
¼ tsp.	–	1.25 ml.
½ tsp.	–	2.5 ml.
1 tsp.	–	5 ml.
1 Tbsp.	–	15 ml.
2 Tbsp. (1 oz.)	1 fl. oz.	30 ml.
¼ cup (2 oz.)	2 fl. oz.	60 ml.
⅓ cup (3 oz.)	3 fl. oz.	80 ml.
½ cup (4 oz.)	4 fl. oz.	120 ml.
⅔ cup (5 oz.)	5 fl. oz.	160 ml.
¾ cup (6 oz.)	6 fl. oz.	180 ml.
1 cup (8 oz.)	8 fl. oz.	240 ml.

Weight Measurements

U.S.	Metric
1 oz.	30 g.
2 oz.	60 g.
4 oz. (¼ lb.)	115 g.
5 oz. (⅓ lb.)	145 g.
6 oz.	170 g.
7 oz.	200 g.
8 oz. (½ lb.)	230 g.
10 oz.	285 g.
12 oz. (¾ lb.)	340 g.
14 oz.	400 g.
16 oz. (1 lb.)	455 g.
2.2 lb.	1 kg.

Length Measurements

U.S.	Metric
¼″	0.6 cm.
½″	1.25 cm.
1″	2.5 cm.
2″	5 cm.
4″	11 cm.
6″	15 cm.
8″	20 cm.
10″	25 cm.
12″ (1′)	30 cm.

Pan Sizes

U.S.	Metric
8″ cake pan	20 x 4-cm. sandwich or cake tin
9″ cake pan	23 x 3.5-cm. sandwich or cake tin
11″ x 7″ baking pan	28 x 18-cm. baking pan
13″ x 9″ baking pan	32.5 x 23-cm. baking pan
2-qt. rectangular baking dish	30 x 19-cm. baking pan
15″ x 10″ baking pan	38 x 25.5-cm. baking pan (Swiss roll tin)
9″ pie plate	22 x 4 or 23 x 4-cm. pie plate
7″ or 8″ springform pan	18 or 20-cm. springform or loose-bottom cake tin
9″ x 5″ loaf pan	23 x 13-cm. or 2-lb. narrow loaf pan or paté tin
1½-qt. casserole	1.5-liter casserole
2-qt. casserole	2-liter casserole

Temperatures

Farenheit	Centigrade	Gas
140°	60°	–
160°	70°	–
180°	80°	–
225°	110°	–
250°	120°	½
300°	150°	2
325°	160°	3
350°	180°	4
375°	190°	5
400°	200°	6
450°	230°	8
500°	260°	–